# KNOWING
## THE WILL OF
# GOD

### BRUCE WALTKE
#### WITH JERRY MACGREGOR

HARVEST HOUSE PUBLISHERS
Eugene, Oregon 97402

*Cover by Left Coast Design, Portland, Oregon*

**KNOWING THE WILL OF GOD**
Copyright © 1998 by Bruce Waltke and Jerry MacGregor
Published by Harvest House Publishers
Eugene, Oregon 97402

Library of Congress Cataloging-in-Publication Data

Waltke, Bruce K.
    Knowing the will of God for the decisions of life / Bruce K. Waltke and Chip MacGregor.
        p.   cm.
    ISBN 1-56507-933-7
    1. Decision-making—Religious aspects—Christianity. 2. God—Will.
3. Christian life. I. MacGregor, Chip, 1958–   .
II. Title.
BV4509.5.W35    1998
248.4—dc21                                                          98-6163
                                                                              CIP

**Printed in the United States of America.**

98 99 00 01 02 03 / BP / 10 9 8 7 6 5 4 3 2 1

*To my wise daughter,*
*Susan Giannini,*
*who brings joy to her parents*
*(Proverbs 10:1)*

BW


*For Mike Allison,*
*who loves Christian books and*
*Christian thinking.*

JCM

# CONTENTS

# PART ONE

# Right and Wrong Concepts

# WHAT IS GOD'S WILL?

▼

*My relationship with God is based on my obedience.*

CHAPTER ONE

$\mathcal{M}$ARGARET IS A SUCCESSFUL career woman with a desire to please God. She worked her way up to a supervisor's position in the accounting division at First National Bank and married rather late in life. Now in her late thirties, she is struggling with the importance of her job. She would like to do something significant for Christ, but feels that her job prevents her from making any changes. Margaret's church recently held a missionary conference in which the speaker challenged Christians to become involved in world evangelism and encouraged everyone to justify why they are not "serving the Lord overseas." Those words stay with Margaret as she ponders spending the next 25 years at her desk, doing the same old accounting tasks.

The next day she reads in the paper about a hurricane devastating the Marshall Islands. The accompanying photograph of two children crying over the death of their parents vividly captures the destruction and deprivation, and

Margaret prays for those poor souls left to fend for themselves. That very afternoon a coworker, making plans for his vacation, leaves a brochure on the Marshall Islands and decides to pray that the Lord would make His will clear to her. That night her husband comes home complaining that the best lawyer in his office, a young man named *Marshall*, has just been transferred to their East Coast office.

"Honey," Margaret says to her husband, "I've been thinking about what that speaker said in church yesterday, and the funniest set of coincidences occurred. Do you think God could be calling us to be missionaries in the Marshall Islands?"

• • •

Dave is a surveyor for a land development firm, with designs to go back to college. He married young and started his family right away, so he never found the time to attend more than a course here and there. But quitting his job isn't very realistic. He's got two kids in school and car payments, and he and his wife have been talking for a long time about getting together a down payment for a home of their own. Still, Dave would like to get training which would better equip him for a career in the long term, and he would also like to take a couple of Bible classes. At a men's breakfast at his church he shares his thoughts with his good friend Tom, who is an older, more experienced Christian. "Have you prayed much about this," his friend asks, "so that you can be given the mind of God?"

"Well, not as much as I'd like," Dave admits.

"Listen," Tom replies, "We're going to pray right now. I want you to make your mind blank. When we're done praying, I want you to tell me the first thoughts the Lord puts into your mind. Okay?"

Dave agrees, and both men pray earnestly. After Tom closes with the words, "Please tell my brother Dave what Your will is," they open their eyes and look at each other. "What's He telling you?"

"I guess that I should be going back to school," Dave replies, wondering if he has really heard the voice of God.

• • •

Suzanne needs direction from the Lord. She has saved a little money, and wants to invest it for her retirement. Since her husband died, she hasn't had anyone she feels she can lean on for sound advice. A nice young man from her church visited Suzanne recently and talked about annuities and other investment strategies, but much of it was over her head. She has also heard from her alma mater, which is looking for people to invest in their child-hood education program, and several Christian organizations have appealed to her for gifts'. Not knowing what to do, Suzanne sits down in her favorite chair, her Bible in her lap.

"I need You to tell me what to do, Lord," she prays silently. "Show me through Your Word." Then she picks up her Bible, flips it open to a page, and begins reading.

"But Jesus said, 'Let the children alone, and do not hinder them from coming to me . . . for the kingdom of heaven belongs to such as these.'" Suzanne takes this as God's leading that she is to invest in children's ministries, and she decides to send her money to the college.

• • •

Douglas is a teenager, active in his youth group at church, and anxious to obey the Lord Jesus. He knows that

Scripture calls him to heed the will of God, but he isn't sure what God's will is for his social life. So Douglas has worked out a system for Friday nights.

First he makes a list of the girls he wants to take out on a date. Then he begins phoning, starting at the top of the list. If the line is busy, he takes that as God's sign that he is not to date that girl. If no one answers, he is to wait and try again later. If the phone rings and the gal he's interested in answers, that means God has given His blessing for Douglas to ask her out.

## Does God Hide His Will?

As you read through these examples, does the thought strike you that perhaps there is some silliness at play in the lives of God's people? The Bible refers to God as our Father, our Provider, and our Redeemer. If we accept the fact that our heavenly Father loves us, and that we are His children, does it make sense that He would hide His will from us? Many Christians talk about "the will of God" as though it were a version of the old con man's ruse, the three-shell game. You remember the game: A pea is hidden under a walnut shell; two other walnut shells are placed on either side of the first, then all three are quickly moved around the table. The con man then asks you, the spectator or "mark," to guess which shell the pea is under. No matter which shell you guess, you are always wrong. You can watch as carefully as possible, trying to unlock the secret of the manipulations, but you can never quite keep up with the manipulator.

When I hear Christians talking about the will of God, they often use phrases such as, "If only I could find God's will," as though He is keeping it hidden from them, or "I'm praying that I'll discover His will for my life," because they apparently believe the Lord doesn't want them to find it, or that He wants to make it as hard as possible for them to find so that they will prove their worth.

Unfortunately, these concepts do not mesh with the balance of Scripture. Isaiah tells us that "there is no one worthy," and the story of the Old Testament is that man, no matter how hard he tries, can never attain to God. If we really believe in God as the perfectly loving Father, we can do away with our notion of Him as an almighty manipulator and con man.

God is not a magician. Our theology tells us that God loves us enough that He sent His Son to die on the cross to pay the penalty for our sins. So does it make sense that He would play some sort of game with His children, hiding His will? Is it logical that the God who says He has a plan for each life would conceal that plan so that His work cannot go forward through His people? It is time for Christians to observe, analyze, and systematically determine what the Bible says about God's will. Perhaps it is time for Christians to ask themselves if the words "finding God's will" are even the best way to phrase the plan the Lord has in mind for each of us.

## A Difficult Term

The term "God's will" is tough to define. It is often used in Scripture to refer to God's eternal plan and decrees: "All the inhabitants of the earth are accounted as nothing, but He does according to His will in the host of heaven and among the inhabitants of earth; and no one can ward off His hand or say to Him, 'What hast thou done?'" (Daniel 4:35 NASB). The will of God refers to his eternal, sovereign rulership over the world that, according to Habbakuk 2:3, "hastens toward the goal, and it will not fail" (NASB). In the New Testament the will of God is sometimes spoken of with reference to His immutable, eternal counsel. Ephesians 1:9-11 reads, "He made known to us the mystery of his will according to his good pleasure, which he purposed in Christ to be put into effect when the times will have reached their fulfillment. . . . In him we are chosen, having been predestined according to the plan of him who works out everything in conformity with the purpose of his will." God has a plan in place, and as that plan is worked out we refer to it as His will.

However, we also use the phrase to describe God's desire or consent—what He wants and what is favorable to Him. "It was not His will," it says in Deuteronomy 10:10, "to destroy you." Isaiah 53:10 tells us "it was the Lord's will" for Christ to suffer for us, and Christ in the Garden of Gethsemane prayed, "Not as I will, but as You will." It is important to grasp this concept of God's will as that which brings Him pleasure, for much of our spiritual growth is learning to live lives pleasing to Him. "It is God's will that you should be sanctified: that you should avoid sexual immorality," says 1 Thessalonians 4:3, and later in that same letter we read, "Give thanks in all circumstances, for this is God's will for you in Christ Jesus" (5:18).

The will of God can refer not only to His immutable decrees and to his pleasures but also to his general providence. King David once said to the whole assembly of Israel, "If it seems good to you, and it is the will of the Lord our God, let us send word far and wide to the rest of our brothers . . . to come and join us" (1 Chronicles 13:2). In effect David is saying, "We do not know the details; providence will have to work it out." Paul took the same approach to God's will in Acts 18:21, telling the Ephesians, "I will come back if it is God's will." The apostle did not know the details of what the future would bring. Paul might or might not return to Ephesus, depending on how events unfolded. If providence favored it, then it must be God's will. James specifically instructed us to pray that way: "You ought to say, 'If it is the Lord's will, we will live and do this or that'" (James 4:15). Sometimes God's will is simply His acts of providence: Whatever comes of our circumstances is God's will.

Finally, we use the term "God's will" to refer to His specific choices in perplexing situations. The Scriptures speak of seeking God's will in some specific situations. It is in this sense that the term is used in the phrase "finding God's will." Moses told his father-in-law that "the people come to me to seek God's will. Whenever they have a dispute, it is brought to me, and I decide between the parties and inform them of God's decrees and laws" (Exodus 18:15,16). God's will is sought in specific decisions, to give us wisdom and guidance. In the early church the disciples, seeking the divine mind in their choice of a new apostle, came before the Lord in perplexity and said, "Show us which of these two you have chosen" (Acts 1:24). Not knowing what they should do, they asked God to make a decision. When we talk of "finding God's will" we generally want divine guidance on specific choices, but it should be noted that this specific term is never used after the Holy Spirit came upon the church at Pentecost. The apostles, upon whom the church is founded, did not teach that we are to seek God's will in this way. Instead, the New Testament offers us a program of the Father's guidance that is based upon having a close relationship with Jesus Christ through the Holy Spirit.

## "Finding" God's Will?

The word "finding" we normally use in the sense of learning or obtaining or attaining to God's mind. When we seek to "find" God's will, we are attempting to discover hidden knowledge by supernatural activity. If we are going to find His will on one specific choice, we will have to penetrate the divine mind to get His decision. "Finding" in this sense is really a form of divination.

This idea was common in pagan religions. As a matter of fact, it was the preoccupation of pagan kings. Most of our texts from the ancient Near East pertain to divination. The king would never act in something as important as going into battle until he had the mind of the god as to whether he should or should not go to war. Many Christians follow this same path in seeking the divine mind in decisions. I have talked with people who perform certain rituals before going to God with an important request, as though they could make themselves more acceptable to God and therefore be more likely to get an answer. But that sort of pagan behavior is what Christ saved us out of. We don't have to slaughter lambs or make great promises or offer special sacrifices as a means of bargaining our way into the presence of God. Christ, with His death on the cross, tore apart the veil in the Holy of Holies. Access to God is no longer limited to one human priest providentially born to the right family, who came to the Lord on behalf of the chosen people. You now have access to God through Jesus Christ. You now have guidance from God through the Holy Spirit. Perhaps the problem is that not enough Christians are walking in close relationship with the God who loves them.

The New Testament gives no explicit command to "find God's will," nor can you find any particular instructions on how to go about finding God's will. There isn't a magic formula offered Christians that will open some mysterious door of wonder, allowing us to get a glimpse of the mind of the Almighty. The Bible forbids pagan divination (Deuteronomy 18:10) and invokes severe penalties for those who resort to magic for determining the will of

God in this way. Simon Magus was severely rebuked in Acts 8 for seeking supernatural powers, and Christ criticized the perverse generation that always asks for a sign from God.

God is not a magic genie. The use of promise boxes, or flipping open your Bible and pointing your finger, or relying on the first thought to enter your mind after a prayer are unwarranted forms of Christian divination.

The reliance on special signs from God is the mark of an immature person—someone who cannot simply believe the truth as presented, but must have a special, miraculous sign as the symbol of authority from God.

## Man's Search for Authority

It is no surprise that we desire to know the mind of God in our specific circumstances. Every person craves wisdom, particularly divine wisdom in the great issues of his or her life. Every person on earth is looking for authority to guide him or her. That is why we talk through tough decisions with friends, colleagues, or parents. We seek assurance—someone to tell us that we are good people, making the right decisions. We want to be seen as not only valuable (something the psychology craze has popularized in recent years) but also competent. I want to know that I'm good at something, that I'm recognized as knowing something important, and that perhaps through my competency I can leave an impact on my world.

Above all that, we fear making a mistake. For you see, a mistake suggests that I am not a competent, worthwhile person. Therefore I will go to extreme measures to make sure that any major decision I make will be a good one. Also, I truly want to please God, so I will seek to discover His mind on the matter at hand.

Unfortunately, our Western culture doesn't offer a strong structure for authority. Parents no longer arrange marriages, and fathers rarely mentor their sons to take over the family craft, so each individual is stuck making his or her own choices. The breakup of the family has taken a toll on the ability of families to communicate, so it seems there is less and less intergenerational wisdom being passed from one generation to the next. The general lack of respect for authority that grew out of the 1960s mindset has also accounted for the lack of contact between generations. Consequently we are seeing young people make choices for which they are unprepared, and often making terrible ones.

So we have the desire for authority, yet a social structure that mitigates against authority in our lives. That motivates believers to seek a divine authority to assist them in making wise choices. Yet their spiritual immaturity often causes them to seek guidance from God in improper ways. It also occasionally puts people in my office at Regent College who think that the way to determine the will of God is to go to an institution of higher learning and learn more about Him. I have often had young people in my office asking, "Is it God's will for me to be at Regent?" to which I can only reply, "What do you mean by God's will?" I want to know the student's walk with God, motives, and ambitions; I do not want to serve as a shill for a school. Occasionally I have had to say to a student, "You're here because you don't know what else to do. You're hiding out, which is more an escape from God than it is a love for Him."

In my view, ministry is a calling, and God not only puts a burning desire in the heart of the learner, but also places people around the student who encourage them to use their gifts in the church. When I see a student without the gifts necessary to pastor, and without the affirmation of the body of Christ, I believe I am looking at a young person who has made some irresponsible choices.

## Divining the Will of God?

Far too many Christians rely on faulty logic to divine the will of God. Their thinking goes like this: "God has a plan, and therefore He intends that I find it." That is a non sequitur, a conclusion that cannot be logically follow the premise. Simply because God has a plan does not mean that He necessarily has any intention of sharing it with you; as a matter of fact the message of Job is in part that the Lord in His sovereignty may allow terrible things to happen to you, and you may never know why. In North America we live such safe and scheduled lives that we come to presume that God will act "fairly" toward us. Then when some young person dies in a tragic accident we cry, "Unfair! How could a loving and just God allow this to happen?" This is an excellent question, and one that Job asked, but he was never given the sort of answer he expected. However, if we contrast our lives with those of Christians living in sections of Africa that have experienced racial strife or who have gone through severe drought, we begin to remember that there is no guarantee of "fairness" in Scripture this side of the grave.

Instructively, the outcomes of faith for the first three heroes of faith celebrated in Hebrews 11 vary considerably. Abel believed God, and he died; Enoch believed God, and he did not die; Noah believed God, and everybody else died! The only thing they had in common is that they believed God and it pleased Him.

The problem of suffering, such as Abel's, leads people to think that either a) there is no God, and life is a pathetic joke, or b) God is a cruel and arbitrary God who cares nothing for the people of earth, or c) God is powerless, or

d) God is alive and at work in our lives, but we do not completely understand Him. It takes faith to believe in the latter concept—something that many people refuse to exercise. But the Bible is clear, and according to Romans 1 nature itself demonstrates that God is alive and powerful, that He loves us, and that He has a plan for everyone. Because God is far beyond what our finite minds can comprehend, we do not know everything about Him nor are we able to always discern His plan. Yet our faith should continue in Him. As Job put it, "Though He slay me, yet will I trust Him."

That's why my following of God is based upon my *relationship* with Him rather than on a special "sign." Rather than looking for some sort of wrapped spiritual package from the Almighty, I want to rely upon my closeness to Him. So when I wonder about which job offer to take, I don't go through a divination process to discover the hidden message of God. Instead I examine how God has called me to live my life, what my motives are, what He has given me a heart for, where I am in my walk with Christ, and what God is saying to me through His Word and His people.

## The "Hunch" Method

I have observed Christians making major decisions based upon the faulty notion that God has a hidden will He wants them to discover, and it has often led to disaster. One couple I know quit their jobs and went into a specialized ministry based on a "hunch" that God wanted them to make a change. I certainly believe the Lord gives us desires and inclinations, but we need to examine our motives behind them. The couple should have spent time discussing their love for God. When you clarify your love for God, and you stand right and clean before Him, it becomes much easier to see how the desires of your own heart match up to those of God. It is certainly cheaper and easier to say, "I've got a feeling," but it lacks the necessary depth and relationship that the Lord uses to shape His people.

Too many people have the used the "hunch" method to rationalize poor decisions or excuse their carnal living. "God told me to buy this expensive home even though it is beyond my financial ability" is certainly convenient for assuaging one's conscience, but it also happens to run in direct contradiction to God's own Word as given to us in the Bible. This sort of cheap reasoning requires no character development at all. God doesn't change you; you simply change your mind. "Wisdom" in the Old Testament is a character trait, not simply thinking soberly. People with wisdom have the character to make good decisions. They don't have to rely on faulty logic.

## The Exegesis Issue

Not only is the logic of many Christians faulty, but their exegesis is terrible. Countless times I have heard people quote Proverbs 3:5,6 as a basis for divining God's will: "Trust in the LORD with all thine heart, and lean not unto thine own understanding. In all thy ways acknowledge him, and he shall direct thy paths" (KJV). Many people read the word "direct" and assume that this verse means God will give them special direction in the everyday decisions of life. But the Hebrew word literally means to "go straight," so a sound exegesis reveals that if you trust God you will not go outside the bounds of what the book of Proverbs teaches. When it says that "he shall direct thy paths" it does not mean that God will offer you special revelation, but that He will make your track right because you are living your life in accordance with the words of Proverbs. Using a verse as a magic incantation does not mean that God is obliged to hand you the answer to your problem. This is simply not true to Christian experience. Receiving a message from God is nearly always in conjunction with having a loving heart toward God. The Spirit of God in your life, together with the influence of the Word, illuminates the thoughts of the Lord. As you put God's Word into practice, He establishes your thoughts so that you can participate in His eternal plan.

Any time you take the Bible out of context you destroy the intent of God's Word. That's why you cannot take instances of special revelation and make them normative for the Christian experience. Paul saw a great light, fell to the ground, and was blinded when he met Jesus Christ. It was an amazing encounter, but if we try to make this experience the norm for all new Christian experiences, we leave most believers out of the kingdom of God. By the same token, the apostle Paul took the gospel message to much of Asia Minor without ever having a specific divine intervention. When he did experience a special revelation, seeing a vision of a man calling him to Macedonia, he obeyed. But the special revelation of God was a rare and unique experience, even for Paul.

The disciples obeyed their calling to preach the good news in Jerusalem, Judea, Samaria, and the uttermost part of the world, but they did so as they were given an opportunity. There are few instances of divine intervention like that of Philip being transported to a new location. And when God did miraculously intervene and lead someone to a special task, it was significant enough to be recorded in Scripture. We cannot take special circumstances and make them the norm by which we live our lives. Special revelation for guidance was not the normal apostolic experience. *And at the time it was received (by Paul, by*

*Philip, by Peter as he lay on his roof) it was not being sought.*

God intervened to change the course of their lives in a dramatic way, not simply tell them to alter their plans a bit. Special revelation came at a time when God wanted to lead them apart from the normal ways in which His people make choices.

There is no place in the New Testament where we are taught to seek a special revelation, and the practice may actually lead to disobedience if it causes us to neglect the everyday opportunities that life brings us in order to wait for a special word from the Lord.

Having said that, I do believe in special revelation, and I do think that too many conservative scholars have no place for God's special intercession because they have no control over it. We can't force God to talk, yet sometimes He completely surprises us and talks anyway.

## The Example of Abraham

One of the most amazing stories in Scripture appears in Genesis 22. Abraham, who has waited decades for God to fulfill His promise and give Abraham a son, can finally rejoice in the birth of Isaac. It will be through Isaac that a great nation will be born, and a Redeemer will come, and the world will be blessed. Abraham is filled up with love for his son and joy in his God. Finally he can see the beginning of a great fulfillment.

Then everything changes. God says, "Take your son, your only son Isaac, whom you love, and go to the region of Moriah. Sacrifice him there as a burnt offering on one of the mountains I will tell you about" (Genesis 22:2).

Imagine the horror of Abraham. He is an old man and won't be having any more sons. It is sad when a father dies and leaves the son behind, but how much sadder when the son dies and leaves the father behind. It is sad when an old man dies and his staff is left behind, but how much sadder for the staff to be taken away. Abraham is told to break his staff. The command seems to be illogical. More than that, it seems absurd. The fulfillment of God's promise that "in Isaac your seed shall be called" is going to disappear. The new hope after many years of disappointed hope is going to be negated.

Beyond that is the revulsion of sacrificing a human being to the one true God, an action associated with pagan deities. On one level it appears that God's order violates His command not to take innocent life. We can rationalize the order by recognizing the truth that "whatever opens the womb belongs to God" (see Exodus 13:11-15). At the least we must say that the order is unconventional and contradicts the custom of Israel. Nevertheless, Abraham knew he must obey the Lord's word. Indeed, this passage is generally studied with an eye toward obedience, but inherent in the story is the concept of God's leading of His people. Average Christians would rebel. "God would never call me to kill my son," they would rationalize. "I must be mistaken. Give me some further sign that I need to make this sacrifice." But Abraham completed this bizarre tale by doing exactly what God called him to do. He was so aware of the special nature of this event that he recognized the importance of complete obedience.

The faith it would take to obey God in this situation amazes me. The fact that God stayed the hand of Abraham, arranging for a replacement sacrifice and blessing the descendants of Isaac, fascinates me. But the idea that the Lord will specially intervene when He must to shape the character of the man teaches me. Abraham did not seek a special message from God. He didn't ask for a sign or demand confirmation from the Lord. He simply walked close to God and obeyed His Word. Those two elements continue to be the essential ingredients of a vibrant faith.

# PAGANS AND THE WILL OF GOD

▼

*Everyone wants to know the mind of God.*

## CHAPTER TWO

*E*VERYONE WANTS TO KNOW the mind of God. Men and women who have not prayed in years, when faced with a critical situation, turn to Him for guidance. Belief in God is an innate human characteristic. We know He is there, although sometimes we talk ourselves out of our belief due to our "advanced learning." Paul put it this way:

> The wrath of God is being revealed from heaven against all the godlessness and wickedness of men who suppress the truth by their wickedness, since what may be known about God is plain to them, because God has made it plain to them. For since the creation of the world God's invisible qualities—his eternal power and divine nature—have been clearly seen, being understood from what has been made, so that men are without excuse (Romans 1:18-20).

## The Worldwide Evidence for God

God can be seen in nature. All a person has to do is look at the universe and he can see a design, a structure, a creation made of intelligence. The psalmist put it this way: "The heavens declare the glory of God; the skies proclaim the work of his hands. Day after day they pour forth speech; night after night they display knowledge. There is no speech or language where their voice is not heard. Their voice goes out into all the earth, their words to the end of the world" (Psalm 19:1-4).

There is an element of intelligence, of purposeful tendency, in the universe. Its order and harmony are marks of a creative intelligence, since order and harmony are invariably conjoined with intelligence. Einstein said that what is incomprehensible from the atheistic position is that the universe is comprehensible. How can the best human minds discern the scientific laws that govern the universe unless a lawgiver decreed them? An examination of a single molecule, with its perfect mathematical and geometrical relationship, is just one illustration of our world's design. God exists, and His existence is evident in nature.

Human beings are possessed of personal being, another argument for the existence of God. We are self-aware and not self-caused, which means that man must have been caused by someone other than ourselves who had sufficient power to produce us as personal spirits. Humankind certainly was caused either by a personal or an impersonal agency, and reason tells us that the cause must be adequate to produce the observed effect. This leads us to believe in a personal, creative God. The element of humanity's mental, moral, and emotional nature must be included in the cause of his creation. Since humankind has an intellectual and moral nature, his Creator must be an intellectual and moral Being. Since you have an emotional nature, only a being of emotion could create you. Your conscience, that part of you which feels guilty over sin and feels compelled toward an ideal, cries out for the existence of a Creator.

As one author puts it, "Some things are wrong, others are right. Love is right, hatred is wrong. Nor is a thing right because it pleases, or wrong because it displeases. Where did we get this standard of right and wrong? Morality is obligatory, not optional. Who made it obligatory? We must believe that there is a God, or believe that the very root of our nature is a lie." [1]

People simply know that God exists. Every culture has naturally believed in a supreme being. And yet some cultures have decided to elevate man and deny the existence of God. Emil Durkheim, in his book *The Elementary Forms of the Religious Life,* studied a primitive tribe in Australia in order to explain how a culture develops its concept of God. He found that as the culture came into being, the people became cognizant of certain desirable social traits, the characteristics that make up the shared social values. Durkheim noticed that these certain traits were communicated from one generation to the next, and inculcated into the conscience of the people. These traits, which sociologists called the "dominant cultural values," reflected not only what the people believed to be good, but also the supernatural source of all things good. Eventually, according to Durkheim, they came to be symbolized by certain animals. If strength was the greatest value, they would depict a bear. If cleverness was dominant, they would depict a fox. If wisdom, an owl.

When these animals were used to symbolically depict a culture's values, they were called totems, from which we in North America get totem poles—carvings of animals with supernatural powers. The totem pole symbolizes the tribe and the values it incarnates. Eventually the tribe comes to worship the animal, which is nothing more than a symbolic representation of its own values and traits. The animal becomes venerated as an object of worship, even though it is merely a representation of what the tribe perceives is worthwhile to possess. That led Durkheim to say that the tribe, in revering the totem, is merely worshiping itself. Their God is themselves.

Emil Durkheim thus came to the conclusion that belief in God is simply a process whereby a group of people, searching for answers to the unknown, come to worship their own external traits. Seeking a way to honor the Creator, they end up worshiping that which was created.

The apostle Paul came to that same conclusion, following up his thoughts on the evidence of God in nature with a stern rebuke:

> For although they knew God, they neither glorified him as God nor gave thanks to him, but their thinking became futile and their foolish hearts were darkened. Although they claimed to be wise, they became fools and exchanged the glory of the immortal God for images made to look like mortal man and birds and animals and reptiles. . . . They exchanged the truth of God for a lie, and worshiped and served the created things rather than the Creator—who is forever praised (Romans 1:21-23,25).

Man knows that God exists, and he wants to be in relationship with Him. Man wants to discern the mind of God, gain His wisdom on events and circumstances of the day, and be exposed to the creative genius of the universe. Consequently, history is full of man's desperate search for God's mind. As I stated earlier, most ancient texts still extant deal with divining the mind of God. Nearly 80 percent of the ancient writings we have simply offer details and prescriptions for determining God's leading. It was the preoccupation of the ancient rulers, who feared the retribution of a god disobeyed. They developed any number of methods for discerning the will of their gods.

## Casting Lots

One form of divination used to penetrate the divine mind was to cast lots, probably a small stone or pebble of some sort. Jonah 1:7 offers an excellent example of how pagans believed this method: "Then the sailors said to each other, 'Come, let us cast lots to find out who is responsible for this calamity.'" The sailors wanted a specific instruction from the Lord as to whom among them was guilty and worthy of punishment, so their way of seeking the hidden information was to cast lots.

One of the things that is often missed by people who study the will of God is the relationship of God to pagans. Because pagan cultures understood the existence of God, it allowed them some openness to the actions of the one true God. Take, for instance, the case of Pharaoh in his dealings with Joseph. Pharaoh recognized not only the wisdom of Joseph in interpreting his dreams, but also the obvious supernatural power behind it. "Since God has made all this known to you, there is no one so discerning and wise as you," Pharaoh admits to Joseph in Genesis 41:39. The fact that God had given Joseph special knowledge was obvious to everyone, and this pagan king acknowledged that fact.

Abimelech and his dealings with Abraham are another example of pagans who can recognize the hand of God. Thinking Sarah is Abraham's sister, King Abimelech takes her as his own. But God Himself comes to Abimelech in a dream, explains the situation, and tells him specifically how to remedy the situation. Abimelech obeys God, and even experiences the healing power of God in Genesis chapter 20. The fact is that most of the pagans lived by the fear of God. They all had an innate moral conscience that allowed them to determine right from wrong. Throughout the Old Testament we see examples of pagan kings performing wickedness and falling out of God's favor, but by the same token we can find examples of pagan kings exercising justice in the eyes of God.

King Nebuchadnezzar not only recognized the power of the true God at work in Daniel, but he also was able to live through a difficult experience that came from turning away from God. Chapter 4 of Daniel tells the story of a pagan king who was filled with pride at his own accomplishments and was turned into a beast for his sin. But at the end of the story Nebuchadnezzar tells us:

> I, Nebuchadnezzar, raised my eyes toward heaven, and my sanity was restored. Then I praised the Most High; I honored and glorified him who lives forever. His dominion is an eternal dominion; his kingdom endures from generation to generation. All the people of the earth are regarded as nothing. He does as he pleases with the powers of heaven and the peoples of the earth. No one can hold back his hand or say to him, "What have you done?"
>
> At the same time that my sanity was restored, my honor and splendor were returned to me for the glory of my kingdom. My advisers and nobles sought me out, and I was restored to my throne and became even greater than before. Now I, Nebuchadnezzar, praise and exalt and glorify the King of heaven, because everything he does is right and all his ways are just. And those who walk in pride he is able to humble (Daniel 4:34-37).

The pagans could and did worship God. Yet they usually worshiped many gods and attributed much of the natural world to the influence of the supernatural. To discover that supernatural wisdom for the issues they faced they would cast lots, having faith in the gods to superintend the answer of the lot.

## Looking for Signs

Pagans devised all sorts of special tasks to help them determine the mind of God. Each of these tasks included searching for some special sign given by the gods. The most popular was *hepatoscopy,* the study of the liver. Pagans believed that memory and intelligence resided in the liver, not the brain, and they created an entire course of study to read livers. The liver was the heaviest organ, and therefore if God was going to reveal His mind to man He would do so through the heaviest and supposedly most important organ.

This may not be as incredible as it first sounds. Earlier in this century we had "phrenologists", who studied the brain's wrinkles and protuberances to determine the character of the individual. Likewise the ancient priests studied the liver and intestines to determine the mind of the gods. The ancient priests would sacrifice a sheep, and "read" the liver's shape to see what God had to say to them, much as a carnival gypsy might read your palm at the fair. One of the greatest kings of Assyria, Ashurbanipal, spent much of his life studying livers in order to divine the will of his god. Most of the ancient texts offer explanations for reading the liver of a sacrificed animal, and they include special notations for encountering unique situations.

The ancients saw hepatoscopy as being particularly important, especially in times of war or famine. It was not unusual for a team of priests to slaughter a dozen sheep and study their livers, hoping to find similar signs in several animals. They felt that the use of many livers, with the work being done by a number of different priests, assured them of a measure of certainty in their work.

As silly as it may seem to us now, this was common practice. The people put much faith in hepatoscopy because they all recognized that there is a God, and they all wanted to communicate with Him. Since the shedding of blood and the very thought of life was wrapped up in a sacrifice, they thought it would offer them a sign from God. It was certainly more bloody, but theoretically not much different, than a modern man or woman who asks God for a sign to guide them. Both are methods of divination that require God to work in a miraculous way to reveal His will.

Another method of looking for a sign was that of *rhabdomancy,* the use of arrows as a sign from the Lord. An example of this occurs in Ezekiel 21:21: "For the king of Babylon will stop at the fork in the road, at the junction of two roads, to seek an omen: He will cast lots with arrows, he will consult his idols, he will examine the liver." The king, unsure of which road his armies must take to conquer the holy land, used three different forms of divination to make up his mind. There were various ways to use arrows in determining the will of God. They could be cast, or tossed, to see which way they pointed. This may seem like nothing more than an ancient equivalent of spinning a lottery wheel, and that would be a valid analogy. But the people of that day believed in the superintendence of the gods in all matters, so even the direction of dropped arrows could not be chalked up to mere chance. As a matter of fact, at least once in history a king turned his soldiers around and refused to attack the enemy because, even though he had superior forces, the arrows strongly suggested a retreat.

*Teraphim,* the use of household idols, is one other method of looking for a sign from God. Making sacrifices to idols was a common practice, and the people hoped to intercede for themselves and gain the favor of the gods. Scripture is very clear about how God's people are to respond to idols: "Do not turn to idols or make gods of cast metal for yourselves. I am the LORD your God" (Leviticus 19:4). We have a jealous God who does not want His people involved with any sort of idol worship. "All who make idols are nothing, and the things they treasure are worthless. Those who would speak up for them are blind; they are ignorant, to their own shame. Who shapes a god and casts an idol, which can profit him nothing?" (Isaiah 44:9,10). Idols were usually statues of a god, sometimes in the form of an animal or other being, although Scripture makes clear that anything which inspires our devotion can be an idol. After trying to please the idol, questions would be asked of it and the people would await the idol's reply.

## The Treachery of Idol Worship

God's people are never to be involved with idols. The prophet Hosea criticized the people of his day by saying, "They consult a wooden idol and are answered by a stick of wood. A spirit of prostitution leads them astray; they are unfaithful to their God" (Hosea 4:12). Jonah adds, "Those who cling to worthless idols forfeit the grace that could be theirs" (Jonah 2:8). That's why the people of Israel were so reviled. Rather than worshiping the various gods of the pagan cultures, they held to their belief in the one true God. And when the nation turned away from worshiping God and began chasing after pagan deities, the country's problems began. "What agreement is there between the temple of God and idols? For we are the temple of the living God. As God has said: "I will live with them and walk among them, and I will be their God, and they will be my people" (2 Corinthians 6:16).

The Bible tells us that when people bow down to worship an idol, they are actually worshiping a demon. "They sacrificed to demons," we read in Deuteronomy 32:17, "which are not God—gods they had not known, gods that recently appeared, gods your fathers did not fear." Paul, writing to the church at Corinth, teaches us that "the sacrifices of pagans are offered to demons, not to God, and I do not want you to be participants with demons" (1 Corinthians 10:20). Satan is behind all idol worship, since it is a means of turning people away from the true God. So anytime an individual worships at an idol, he is actually worshiping Satan. That's why Paul commends the Thessalonians for being people who "turned to God from idols to serve the living and true God" (1 Thessalonians 1:9), and why the apostle John warns his flock to "keep yourselves from idols" (1 John 5:21).

Anytime a believer gets into a behavior pattern where he performs some activity to gain God's pleasure, then awaits His word through some obscure sign, I believe he is in very treacherous waters. Certainly Christians who use their Bibles like a magic book, letting it fall open to a page and randomly pointing to a verse, come dangerously close to idol worship. And those who use a promise box, with various Scripture verses written on cards that are pulled out at random to speak to the need of the moment, behave like those involved in teraphim. We should stay away from that sort of divination. We are no longer pagans, and we should have nothing to do with these pagan behaviors.

## Watching the Stars

About the sixth century B.C. *astrology* made its debut. Priests and other learned men believed they could determine the divine mind by reading the stars, and they created elaborate systems for doing so. The prophet Isaiah, writing to comfort the exiles in Babylon, mocks the astrologists in Isaiah 47:13: "Let your astrologers come forward, those stargazers who make predictions month by month." The premise behind astrology was originally that the stars, as the celestial home of God, would reveal His mind. Later the harmony of science led astrologists to believe that the eternal purposes of God would be evident in the message of the heavens.

Based upon the observations and the traditions of the centuries, astrologers claim that certain heavenly phenomena are synchronous with earthly circumstances. The movements of the planets are believed to influence the events of mankind. The heavens are divided into 12 sections, called "houses," and as the planets pass through each section they form geometrical patterns, known as "aspects," which exert a beneficial or troublesome influence. By plotting the signs under which a person was born, an astrologer creates a horoscope that summarizes the individual's personalities and tendencies. When this information is applied to a particular date, the astrologer claims to offer specific predictions regarding success, failure, warnings, opportunities, and the like.

Astrology gained much favor during the Hellenistic age, offering a supposedly more precise method of determining the will of God. The introduction of the Julian calendar made astrological computation easy, and people from all walks of life began to depend upon horoscopes. Emperor Tiberius made decisions in accordance with his horoscope, and intellectuals throughout history have found astrology's claim of universal harmony appealing. However, modern astronomy, in revealing the vastness of the universe, has shown the lack of information available to those drawing up astrological charts and the implausibility of anyone relying on them for important decisions.

Having said that, two York University professors have found that 45 percent of first-year university students studying the liberal arts believe there is something to astrology, and that 20 percent have made at least one decision in the past year based on their horoscope. Even more astonishing is that 37 percent of those studying the hard sciences at the university hold some belief in astrology, telling the researchers that astrologers can "predict one's character and future by studying the heavens." Michael De Robertis, who along with Paul Delaney conducted the study, said the survey reveals how science and mathematics courses in public high schools have failed. "In education we should be teaching students what real life is all about. . . . They don't know that statistically there is nothing to [astrology] and there never has been anything to it."[2]

Newspapers across America publish an astrological chart every day, and while we think them silly nonsense, interest in them is growing. In the 1980s Nancy Reagan made headlines by revealing that she became caught up in her horoscope, even making recommendations to the President on what actions to take based upon the stars!

Scripture clearly warns against depending on astrologers and any other diviner. Second Kings 17:16 warns of people who "forsook all the commands of the Lord their God and made for themselves two idols cast in the shape of calves, and an Asherah pole. They bowed down to the starry host and they worshipped Baal." Later in that same book we read of King Josiah ordering the high priest "to remove from the temple of the LORD all the articles made for Baal and Asherah and all the starry hosts" and to do away with the pagan priests, "those who burned incense to Baal, to the sun and moon, to the constellations and to all the starry hosts" (2 Kings 23:4,5). The prophet Jeremiah warns us, "This is what the LORD says: 'Do not learn the ways of the nations or be terrified by the signs in the sky, though the nations are terrified by them. For the customs of the people are worthless'" (Jeremiah 10:2,3).

## Telling Your Fortune

One of the oldest forms of determining the will of God for an individual's future was by *hydromancy,* or using water to tell fortunes. If you remember the story of Joseph having a steward hide his cup in his brother Benjamin's sack, the cup itself was noteworthy. In Genesis 44:5 we read, "Isn't this the cup my master drinks from and also uses for divination?" His statement is sarcastic. The ancient believed they could read the liquid left in a bowl, and that it would predict the future of the person who used it. It is the same principle as reading tea leaves or mixing tarot cards, believing that a person's "karma" somehow significantly influences all that he touches.

Much of our modern New Age religion is based upon this principle of divine influence in everyday articles. People who worship the earth, those who believe in reincarnation, and the growing interest in universal harmony all stem from this same idea that there is a mixing of the spiritual and the physical that can be attained by those who study it. Nearly all of the New Age movement is focused on trying to attain some hidden knowledge of God, with the hope that this knowledge will change both

37

the individual and the world. Books, tapes, and seminars preach a pantheistic message of finding supernatural power that fills the spiritual void of the individual.

I find it amazing how much New Age thinking has influenced our society. The compromise and toleration of evil in our social morality, the growth of nature-worship groups, and the friendly reception these ideas receive in the media suggest a society starved for spiritual truth but undiscriminating in its taste. Regrettably, the postmodern thinkers gain some credibility because they bestow rights on animals. If the church had paid more attention to the rights God bestowed on animals, as for example in the Ten Commandments, granting the animals a sabbatical rest, it would have deprived them of this moral credibility.

The sale of tarot cards, Ouija boards, and crystal balls has skyrocketed in recent years. Those writing books on seeking the will of God by meditation or hallucinogenic drugs are getting rich. And the fable that man can somehow tell the future continues to intrigue the gullible.[3]

## Talking with Spirits

God laid down the law with Israel:

> Do not practice divination or sorcery. . . . Do not turn to mediums or seek out spiritists, for you will be defiled by them (Leviticus 19:26,31).

> Let no one be found among you who . . . practices divination or sorcery, interprets omens, engages in witchcraft, or casts spells, or who is a medium or spiritist or who consults the dead. Anyone who does these things is detestable to the LORD (Deuteronomy 18:10-12).

> They practiced divination and sorcery and sold themselves to do evil in the eyes of the LORD, provoking him to anger (2 Kings 17:17).

> When men tell you to consult mediums and spiritists, who whisper and mutter, should not a people inquire of their God? Why consult the dead on behalf of the living? (Isaiah 8:19).

The Bible rejects these pagan forms of divination because they imply that some other spiritual power rules the universe than Israel's good, wise, and just God. He rules along the lines of justice, ultimately rewarding the good and punishing the evil. For Christians, Christ's active obedience satisfies God's demands of justice and the Holy Spirit enables them to live righteously and for Christ to live in them.

Throughout history people have turned to prophets, oracles, and seers to help interpret the signs of God. In our own day we have witnessed the rise in phony messiahs and spiritual charlatans who deceive many people, usually getting extremely wealthy in the process. The Baghwan Shree Rajneesh claimed to be divine, but his divinity couldn't stop his death from cancer in his fifties.

L. Ron Hubbard, once a science fiction writer who found his readers believing in the world he created in his stories, started the Church of Scientology and made a fortune selling books full of a strange mix of psychology and theology. The Korean religious leader Sun Moon says he is the incarnation of Jesus Christ, a claim made by dozens of people this century. There is no end of people who claim to have discovered the "new truth," something orthodox Christianity must have missed throughout the centuries.

Not only is there an ever-growing list of cults, but interest in parapsychology and the supernormal is exploding.

Astral projection and channeling claim to put people in touch with the spirits of those long dead, a practice the Bible makes clear God abhors.

With all of this interest in the supernatural, with all of this activity aimed at getting in touch with the will of God, it is amazing how few people seem at peace with the Almighty. The fact is that all of this divination activity has done little more than confuse people. Meanwhile, a loving and patient God waits for His people to turn to Him in obedience.

# GOD'S WILL
# IN THE
▼ # OLD TESTAMENT

*In times past, God has offered guidance to His people.*

## CHAPTER THREE

*F*OR ALL OF THE crazy machinations people have tried in order to get in touch with the divine mind, the fact remains that God has, in times past, offered guidance to His people through instruments for divining His will. There are examples in Scripture where people have divined the hidden will of God for specific situations. As I've already said, pagan forms of divination that subverted dependence upon God and circumvented His laws of justice were disallowed by the Lord. "Let no one be found among you . . . who practices divination," the Lord says in Deuteronomy 18:10. There was to be no magic, no sorcery, no witchcraft or spells, no contacting the dead.

Israel, ideally a nation of ethical monotheists, was a nation who believed that God rules all things according to righteousness. The future of each man and woman was decided upon the basis of God's justice. Each person was held responsible for his or her own life. The way people lived their lives determined their future, not fate or magic.

The saying is true: "What you are now determines what you will be then." To rely on some manner of divination, rather than on the character of God and an individual's relationship to Him is a shortcut. Thus discerning the will of God through pagan forms of divination was forbidden. There were, however, six circumstances in the Old Testament in which God chose to reveal His mind through supernatural means of divination.

## By Prophets

"Formerly in Israel, if a man went to inquire of God, he would say, 'Come, let us go to the seer'" (1 Samuel 9:9). A person in Old Testament times could go to a prophet if he wanted to have God's wisdom on a particular situation. In 1 Samuel chapters 9 and 10 Saul wanted to know where his father's donkeys were, so he went to a seer, the prophet Samuel, who could reveal the location of the animals. Barak went to Deborah the prophetess to determine the course of Israel's war with the Canaanites (Judges 4). Throughout history God has used a few individuals in significant ways to influence the course of nations.

The canonical prophets, whose books make up over a quarter of the Old Testament, were called by God to be channels of revelation. They were men of God who stood in His counsel, knew His mind, and were enabled to declare it. God the Holy Spirit spoke in and through them. They knew He was doing so; hence they dared to begin proclamations with "Thus says the Lord," presenting the LORD Himself as the Speaker of what they were saying.

Prophecy involved prediction (foretelling), but usually this was done in a context of declaring God's warnings and exhortations to His covenant people (forthtelling). The prophets looked forward to the coming of the messianic King and His kingdom after purging judgments, but often their chief concern was exhortation to repentance, in the hope that impending judgments might be averted. The prophets were primarily reformers, enforcing God's law and recalling God's people to the covenant faithfulness from which they had lapsed.

Along with their preaching to the nation went their prayers for the nation—they talked to God about people just as earnestly as they talked to people about God. They fulfilled a unique ministry as intercessors.

False prophets were a bane to Israel. Professionally linked with Israel's organized worship, they said what people wanted to hear and spoke their own dreams and opinions rather than words of God. In the New Testament, one book (Revelation) announces itself as a true and trustworthy prophecy, received directly from God through Jesus Christ. The ministry of the apostles brought instruction directly from God to His people, just as the Old Testament prophetic ministry had done, though the form of presentation was different. The prophets of the New Testament period were linked with the apostles in the foundation of the church as expositors of the fulfillment in Christ of Old Testament prophecy.

God's prophets, unlike pagan prophets, never subverted dependence upon God or circumvented His Word. Moses expressly forbade the people from following a prophet who would do so: "If a prophet, or one who foretells by dreams, appears among you and announces a miraculous sign or wonder, and if the sign or wonder of which he has spoken takes place, and he says 'Let us follow other gods' (gods you have not known), 'and let us worship them,' you must not listen to the words of that prophet or dreamer. The LORD your God is testing you to find out whether you love him with all your heart and with all your soul. . . . That prophet or dreamer must be put to death, because he preached rebellion against the LORD your God" (Deuteronomy 13:1-5).

At Sinai the people had asked Moses to mediate God's words to them. After Moses died, the question arose as to who would continue that responsibility. The Lord revealed that the prophets would replace Moses as mediators of God's righteous words to His people: "The nations you will dispossess listen to those who practice sorcery or [pagan] divination. But as for you, the LORD your God has not permitted you to do so. The LORD your God will raise up for a prophet like me from among your own brothers. You must listen to him. For this is what you asked of the LORD your God at Horeb on the day of the assembly when you said, 'Let us not hear the voice of the LORD our God nor see this great fire anymore'" (Deuteronomy 18:14-16).

## By Urim and Thummim

The priest could use the Urim and Thummim to determine God's will in a particular situation. We are not exactly sure what the Urim and Thummim were, but the priest carried in his breastplate perhaps two sticks or stones, one white and the other black, that would give a yes or no answer to a specific question. Should Israel be preparing for battle, they would somehow shake or toss the sticks. If they turned up black the Israelites would not go to battle, and if they turned up white they would proceed into battle with the knowledge that they were in the will of God. That is one form of divination that God allowed in the Old Testament. We read in Exodus 28:30, "Also put the Urim and Thummim in the breastpiece, so they may be over Aaron's heart whenever he enters the presence of the LORD. Thus Aaron will always bear the means of making decisions for the Israelites over his heart before the LORD." Much has been made of the Urim and

Thummim by modern mystics, who want to find in them the key to the divine mind. All sorts of fanciful explanations have been put forward, including that the items may have glowed, that they had secret words engraved on them, or that they were ancient artifacts with magical powers. However, it should be noted that 1 Samuel 28:6 makes it clear that a definite answer was not always obtainable, so it may not have been as simple as tossing two stones on the ground. Moses never used them; they were given for the high priest in aiding those who could not find God's guidance any other way.

Some scholars translate the words "Urim" and "Thummim" to mean "curse" and "blessing," others simply "dark" and "light," although the literal translation seems to be "lights" and "perfections." There is no proof that they were only two items; some early rabbis believed that the Urim and Thummim were a series of stones with Hebraic characters on them by which the Lord could spell out a message for the high priest. However, most scholars believe them to be two sticks or stones, perhaps precious stones, that God used in a miraculous way to reveal His will. They were used for national decisions like going to war, and for priestly matters.

The Old Testament seems to indicate that the Urim and Thummim faded from use during the early days of Israel's monarchy, and they are only referred to once after the Babylonian exile. This may be so because after the institution of the monarchy, God inaugurated the office of the prophet. The prophets now participated in God's heavenly court and communicated God's messages to the courts in Jerusalem and Samaria. Apparently prophets who revealed God's Word to the king replaced the Urim and Thummim, through which He revealed His mind to the priest. Nevertheless, we still find Ezra using this device to determine the ancestry of the priests who returned from the exile in Ezra chapter 2. After this the Bible never mentions the Urim and Thummim again. God did not preserve it for His people. They were one more allowance from God to assist His people at a certain point in history.

## By Sacred Lot

The decision to parcel out the Holy Land was done through sacred lots: "I will cast lots for you in the presence of the LORD" (Joshua 18:6). However the lot turned out determined how the land was allotted to each tribe of Israel, and it should be noted that the lots turned out exactly as Jacob's prophecies back in Genesis chapter 49 said they would. God used the lot in several Old Testament circumstances to reveal His selection of someone or something when the people were in the dark. For example, a sacred lot was used to distribute goods and booty (Nahum 3:10), to decide upon Saul as king (1 Samuel 10), and to determine the order of priests and their duties (1 Chronicles 24). There are also instances of sacred lot being used to identify the offender from among a group, as was done with Achan in Joshua 7 and with the prophet Jonah in the first chapter of his book.

The story of Jonah being chosen by sacred lot is significant, because it points out how God sometimes ruled even through the casting of lots by pagans. "The lot is cast into the lap," it says in Proverbs 16:33, "but its every decision is from the LORD." A lot was deemed a final decision because it was cast down by God. It appears that a lot was usually resorted to when other forms of wisdom had failed, but the casting of lots ended with the church. The last time it was mentioned in Scripture was in Acts 1:26, when the 11 remaining disciples drew lots to select a replacement for Judas Iscariot. The lot fell to Matthias, who is never heard from again, leading me to believe the lot was no longer useful for the church. Indeed, there is never another recorded use of anyone in Christ's church going before the Lord to cast lots. We have been given God's Word, and His Holy Spirit resides in us, so we do not rely on merely rolling dice.

## By Dreams

God sometimes spoke to people through dreams to reveal His will. He gave Joseph the dream that his brothers would all bow down to him, precipitating a long string of events that would lead to the salvation of his family from famine (Genesis 37ff.). God sent a dream to Gideon's friend, encouraging Gideon to lead Israel into battle with the Midianites (Judges 7). Daniel was given a dream by the Lord that detailed the end of the world (Daniel 7). This is something the Lord continued to do in New Testament times, sending Mary's husband Joseph dreams about the birth of Jesus and the wrath of Herod. He even occasionally sent dreams to pagans such as Abimelech and Nebuchadnezzar, to let them know the reality of their situations. And the Lord promises us through Joel that in the last days, "I will pour out my Spirit on all people. Your sons and daughters will prophesy, your old men will dream dreams, your young men will see visions" (Joel 2:28).

Psychology has been much enamored with dreams ever since Sigmund Freud claimed that they offered a window to the soul. However, it should be noted that Freud worked with World War I veterans, some of whom had seen terrible battles and who experienced violent dreams of war. While there might be something to the idea of the subconscious creatively expressing itself through dreams, much of the literature on interpretation of dreams is so wildly speculative as to be almost laughable. I certainly believe that God can work through my dreams to offer me guidance if He chooses to do so, but I also believe He has offered me better alternatives that I can put into practice to determine His will.

## By Signs

There is no question about it: God occasionally used miraculous signs to get the attention of our ancestors and to guide them. In the Old Testament He sent fire from heaven (Judges 6:15-22), spoke through a burning bush (Exodus 3), and put words into the mouths of the enemy (1 Samuel 14:8-12). In each case an event vital to the life of the nation of Israel was involved, and the Lord moved miraculously to prepare the people and their leaders.

Perhaps the most often cited sign in the Old Testament is that of Gideon and his fleece in Judges chapter 6. The nation of Israel had turned away from God, and as a result had been given into the hands of the Midianites, who ravaged their land. God sent an angel to a young farmer, Gideon, and promised to be with Gideon in his venture to free God's people. Out of unbelief, Gideon asked for a sign of God's presence. To assist his faith, the angel miraculously consumed his sacrificed. He still didn't believe so God miraculously made Gideon's fleece first dry, then wet. Yet, he still did not believe. He believed only after he heard a midianite soldier's dream. He had more faith in the foreigner's dream then in the word of the LORD. In short, the fleece was a part of his unbelief and, as such, is not a model for faith.

This is a great story about God watching out for His people even when their leaders lacked faith. The putting out of a fleece is to be censured and not made normative for making decisions. I have heard Christians speak of "putting out the fleece" on whether to purchase a car, invest in a new product, or select a school. Those kinds of decisions, while certainly important to the individual believer, are not on the same scale with determining the course of a nation whom God has selected for a blessing. God cares for each of us, and desires to walk in a right relationship with Him, but today He does not resort to supernatural signs to move us to action.

The apostles never put out the equivalent of a fleece. Moreover, they never even hinted that Christians should look for "signs" as a means of determining God's will. We should look for signs signaling the end of the age, but that is not the same thing as using signs for "finding God's will." Remember that Jesus promised that the Comforter or Helper, the Holy Spirit, would teach the apostles all things and bring to their remembrance all the things that he had said to them (John 14:26). Jesus never taught His church to use signs in the way Gideon did. The Spirit enlightens (Ephesians 1:17,18), regenerates (John 3:5-8), sanctifies (Galatians 5:16-18), transforms (2 Corinthians 3:18; Galatians 5:22,23), and gives God's people what they need in order to serve Him (1 Corinthians 12:4-11). God leads His people not through signs but through His Word, His Holy Spirit, His church, Christian friends who offer godly counsel, and His providential circumstances.

One of the lessons from the life of Jesus is that people will not turn to God simply because they see a miracle. Instead, they will simply ask for another miracle. So God leaves the miraculous for those few great moments when a miracle is the best way to alter the course of history. Please do not misunderstand me: I *do* believe in a God who can perform miracles, even in our own day. But I don't find that miracles are the course of events for Christian direction, so I think "laying out the fleece" is generally the lazy man's way to discern the will of God. It requires no work, little discipline, and almost no character development. God has a different program of guidance.

## By Words

Finally, sometimes God reveals His will to individuals by speaking to them, either directly or through a messenger. The Lord spoke to Abraham and Moses directly, and even sent His angels to Gideon, Balaam, Manoah, David, Elijah, and Ezekiel. Sometimes the angels bring good news, as when they appeared to the shepherds outside Bethlehem, and sometimes they bring a warning, as when they came to Abraham before destroying Sodom and Gomorrah. Hearing the voice of God in an audition or seeing His messengers in a vision are rare events, and the Bible records them precisely because they are so significant. God is still alive, still at work in our lives, and so He could conceivably speak to us in these ways if He so chose. The angels still do His bidding, so He could certainly send an angel with a message to us, as He did to the disciples as they stood watching Jesus ascend into heaven.

But what would an angel say to twentieth-century North America? Perhaps he would state: "Your nations are replete with the foulest of sin. The Lord helped you set your countries up; He gave you everything you needed to succeed. Why have you turned your back on Him? Judgment is coming." But angels have no need to say that, because many Christians are already saying it clearly. We are turning to paganism and darkness, and morality is slipping away at an alarming rate. Unless there is significant revival, I'm afraid we are doomed to suffer the consequences of our nation's actions. The fact is that we have God's Word, and we proclaim it openly. People are without excuse. I see no reason why God would send an angel in this circumstance.

Recently there has been a movement to claim to have received a "word from the Lord." This practice could possibly be helpful, but it also has some real dangers. If people are not mature and clean before God, I have no interest in hearing any words they claim to be receiving from God. The message can be muddied by the messenger. And if someone has a word from God, am I expected to treat it on par with Scripture? I think not. It would be better if he or she were to say, "I think I have the mind of the Lord." The Canon is closed, and God has given us His complete Word. Of course, I have already admitted that the Lord uses mature Christian friends to guide us at times, so I am willing to allow that He gives wisdom to others and nudges them to share it with me, but I approach the concept of God speaking directly through another person very cautiously.

## Finding God's Will Today

There are no examples of explicitly seeking or finding God's will after Acts 1:24-26, in which the disciples drew lots to select Matthias as a replacement for Judas. There are dreams, visions, and revelations after this, but never in the context of explicitly seeking God's will. From this point onward it is not divination (seeking to probe the divine mind) but revelation given by God to His people. After Pentecost there is no instance of the church seeking God's will through any of the forms of divination listed above.

The problem of using divination today is that the techniques Christians use, like promise boxes and seeking signs, are not examples offered to those living under the New Covenant. So when a believer is told to "not take a job until you have God's mind," I think he may be led astray. His faulty logic and faulty exegesis cause him to believe in divination, but there is no such biblical example to follow for Christians.

Christians are quick to point to James 1:5 as their proof text: "If any of you lacks wisdom, he should ask God, who gives generously to all without finding fault, and it will be given to him." They interpret "wisdom" to mean God's special revelation, and the reasoning goes something like this: If you need special wisdom when making a decision, go to God, consult Him, and wait for Him to give you the answer you're looking for. However, in James the word "wisdom" is not referring to guidance. Wisdom refers to a way of life. James defines wisdom in James 3:13 when he talks about earthly wisdom being self-centered and ambitious. This kind of wisdom is not of God. "But the wisdom that comes from heaven is first of all pure; then peace-loving, considerate, submissive, full of mercy and good fruit, impartial and sincere" (James 3:17). Wisdom is a way of life, revealed in the person's character. So when James says, "If any of you lack wisdom," he is referring to lacking purity, peacefulness, gentleness, and the like. I find the word "wisdom" constantly used out of context in churches. The kind of heavenly wisdom James is talking about is brought to earth through prayer.

God's method of revealing His mind with regard to specific choices in a perplexing situation before Pentecost is not normative for the church. Apart from the lot in Acts 1, the church lacks both prescriptive and perceptual warrant in the New Testament. God does not administer His church in the same way He administered old Israel. He administered old Israel by the Mosaic law, but we are no longer administered by that law. He administers us by the Spirit, not the law, and this changed at Pentecost.

If there were even one verse after Pentecost that talked about divining God's will, then I would be in favor of all this divination business. But there is simply no statement in the New Testament that teaches me to find God's will in this sense, nor can I find any instances in Scripture of the early church practicing divination after the Holy Spirit has come. There is a radical change between the Old Testament and the New Testament practice. So the practice of using the Urim and Thummim, or going to a seer, or casting a sacred lot is no longer valid for New Testament Christians. I don't find any verses recommending the Old Testament practices or making them the norm for New Testament believers. The various leadings in the New Testament by prophets, visions, and angelic visitations never occur in response to attempts to "find God's will."

Therefore I contend that we need to redefine the idea of finding God's will. We need to drop entirely the concept of divination, which is not appropriate for Christians. We should reformulate our ideas and focus on what the Scriptures teach about the way our God guides His elect saints to do His pleasure.

# PART TWO

# God's Program of Guidance

# READ
# YOUR BIBLE

▼

*The wise Christian reads Scripture, meditates on it, and puts it into practice.*

CHAPTER FOUR

*G*OD GUIDES HIS PEOPLE to do His pleasure. It is imperative that we grasp the fact that the Lord guides us rather than hides from us. He doesn't sit back and play games with His children. Instead, He offers us clear guidance for living our lives to please Him. We must learn the concept of following God's program of guidance.

The Lord provides a six-point program of supervised care in directing His elect. *The order of those six steps is very important.* You cannot start in the middle or skip to the end. If you want to be clear on God's guidance for your life, you must begin with the first step, then move to the second. *There is a prioritized sequence for the way He guides His saints, and it begins on the basis of Holy Scripture.*

## Read Regularly

The first step to gaining God's guidance is to read your Bible. Remember the words of Paul to his young friend Timothy:

But as for you, continue in what you have learned and have become convinced of, because you know those from whom you learned it, and how from infancy you have known the holy Sciptures, which are able to make you wise for salvation through faith in Christ Jesus. All Scripture is God-breathed and is useful for teaching, rebuking, correcting and training in righteousness, so that the man of God may be thoroughly equipped for every good work (2 Timothy 3:14-17).

The Scriptures are given to us for our *learning*. That means the Lord gave us the Bible to help us learn how to do things. It offers the believer lessons and instruction on life, so that he may develop skills, knowledge, and insight. God teaches us through His Word.

The Scriptures are also given to us for *rebuke*. God reprimands His people when they turn away from Him. The Bible can clearly show us where we have gotten off the path of truth, and it offers us a warning that we are headed in the wrong direction. The word "rebuke" literally means "to force back," and Scripture forces us to face the truth. Unfortunately, there are times I choose to ignore what God says through His Word because I enjoy my sin and choose to disobey. However, I eventually recognize that I want my life to please God, and, rebuked by His Word, I turn back to Him.

The Scriptures are also given to us for *correcting*. Correction changes something from wrong to right. It rectifies errors and makes us conform to the proper standard. God doesn't merely scold us for making mistakes, but offers correction so that we will not make the same mistake again. The Bible puts us back on the right path, guiding us toward a healthy relationship with the Lord.

The Scriptures are also given to us for *training in righteousness,* so that we can conform our lives to God's standard. The Bible would be a punitive document if it only rebuked and corrected the saints. Fortunately, it also offers information, actions, and exercises that help us grow. It guides our development, preparing us for the new life to which we have been called.

None of these benefits can be reaped if you do not read your Bible. It is God's immediate tool for shaping your life. It is how the Lord chose to reveal Himself to mankind in our day. There is no better way to know and experience God than through His living Word, for it is His fundamental revelation instructing us. For all those who seek to "discover God's will" for their lives, I offer 1 Thessalonians 5:15-18: "See that no one repays another with evil for evil, but always seek after that which is good for one another and for all men. Rejoice always; pray without ceasing; in everything give thanks; for this is God's will for you in Christ Jesus" (NASB).

Do you want to know the will of God for your life? It is to rejoice, pray, give thanks, and seek after that which is good for all men. You can't pass that off as "too simplistic" or "not relevant," either, since this is God's Word offering the answer. God wants you to be a mature man or woman of God—*that is His will for your life!* He wants to see your character develop. He wants you to draw close to Him and be changed. We have the Holy Spirit in a fuller measure than the Old Testament saints, and He develops our character. This is why God terminated the Old Testament means of divination. Divining is a shortcut to the future, and God offers Christians no shortcuts.

Divination sounds pious, but it may actually be ungodly because it shortcuts the Spirit's work in developing our character. It assumes you can know God's mind without having His heart and His Spirit. But discerning the mind of God cannot be done apart from character development. You cannot divine God's heart, but you have available to you a way to develop a heart like His. He can work in your life through the Holy Spirit and His Word to foster virtue, and then you will have the mind of Christ.

Our central revelation, to which we are held accountable, is God's Word to His people. "In the past God spoke to our forefathers through the prophets at many times and in various ways, but in these last days he has spoken to us by his Son, whom he appointed heir of all things, and through whom he made the universe" (Hebrew 1:1,2). Jesus, according to John 1, is the Word incarnate. Words bind people together. By His Word, Jesus Christ, God binds us to Himself. Jesus Christ has given us an example of how we are to live our lives, for He has suffered everything that we suffer. The way we can come to know Him better and follow His example is to read about Him in our Bibles.

We live in a golden age for Christian publishing. Never have so many words been written nor so many pages published on the Lord Jesus Christ. Every city in North America seems to have a Christian bookstore, and their shelves are filled with interesting, helpful, and profound books on the Christian life. The downside of all this is that I think many people have shied away from Scripture itself. There is so much out there, and much of it seems awfully interesting to Christians, so it has become easier to read the latest popular book on God or the church or the family than it is to read the Bible.

Nevertheless, the Bible is the only Book that is God's direct message to us. You must spend time reading God's Word or you will never mature in your Christian faith. I am not suggesting there is anything wrong with reading good Christian books, and I am certainly not criticizing

Christian publishers. I am simply reminding you that all of those good books will amount to very little in your life if you do not spend time in the most important book of all, the Holy Bible.

God guides us as we read His book. The psalmist writes:

> Blessed are they whose ways are blameless,
> who walk according to the law of the LORD.
> Blessed are they who keep his statutes and seek
> him with all their heart.
> They do nothing wrong; they walk in his ways.
> You have laid down precepts that are to be fully
> obeyed.
> Oh, that my ways were steadfast in obeying
> your decrees!
> Then I would not be put to shame when I consider
> all your commands.
> I will praise you with an upright heart as I learn all
> your righteous laws.
> I will obey your decrees; do not utterly forsake me.
> How can a young man keep his way pure?
> By living according to your word.
> I seek you with all my heart; do not let me stray
> from your commands.
> I have hidden your word in my heart that I might
> not sin against you (Psalm 119:1-11).

To the many Christians who spend time trying to divine the will of God, I ask, "How much time have you spent reading the Bible?" To know what pleases God—what His desires are—you must know His heart. And to know His heart you must draw close to Him. Reading His personal message to His people is the best way to know Him. Those serious about their walk with God will spend time listening to His message.

The writer of Psalm 119 goes on to exult in God's Word:

> I delight in your decrees; I will not neglect your
> word  (verse 16).
> Open my eyes that I may see wonderful things in
> your law  (verse 18).
> Your statutes are my delight; they are my counselors
> (verse 24).
> I have chosen the way of truth; I have set my heart
> on your laws (verse 30).
> Direct me in the path of your commands, for there
> I find delight (verse 35).
> How I long for your precepts! Preserve my life in
> your righteousness (verse 40).
> I will speak of your statutes before kings and will
> not be put to shame (verse 46).
> I remember your ancient laws, O LORD, and I find
> comfort in them (verse 52).
> Your word is a lamp to my feet and a light for my
> path (verse 105).
> You are my refuge and my shield; I have put my
> hope in your word (verse 114).
> The unfolding of your words gives light; it gives
> understanding to the simple (verse 130).
> May my cry come before you, O LORD; give me
> understanding according to your word
> (verse 169).

That expresses what our attitude should be toward Scripture. As we take the time to read it, we will learn about God and will be shaped by His Word. Then we will best be able to understand what He desires from us.

## Interpret Properly

Part of reading the Bible is knowing how to interpret it. Every growing Christian should learn to handle the Scripture in a credible way. We must seek accurate interpretations, so that we not only know what the words *say*, but what they *mean*.

The apostle Paul said to Timothy, "The things you have heard me say in the presence of many witnesses entrust to reliable men who will also be qualified to teach others. . . . Do your best to present yourself to God as one approved, a workman who does not need to be ashamed and who correctly handles the word of truth" (2 Timothy 2:2,15). Paul was not just searching for men who were available, but for those who were reliable and who had the ability to teach other people. They were going to have to share God's divine truths with others, and the apostle knew it was imperative that they were able to interpret God's Word correctly.

Unfortunately, the church is full of people who mishandle Scripture, particularly on this issue of God's guidance. I recently heard a Christian talk about Psalm 32:8 ("I will instruct you and teach you in the way you should go") and claim the verse as evidence that we need to look to God for special instruction regarding His will. This leads believers right back into the practice of divination that we talked about earlier in this book. It asks Christians to look for signs from God that will reveal some mysterious secret.

In truth, this Christian imposed his own ideas on the text. The author of Psalm 32 is David, who is speaking to the congregation of Israel. He has just celebrated God's forgiveness, and now he wants to instruct Israel in how they should live. So when he says to the congregation, "I will instruct you and teach you in the way you should go," he means that he, David, will teach them, and that they should "not be like the horse or the mule, which have no understanding but must be controlled by bit and bridle." David is encouraging the nation of Israel to remain obedient to God. He reminds them that the wicked suffer harm, but God's love surrounds the righteous, and he closes his psalm with an exhortation to rejoice and sing.

That same hermeneutic misinterprets Proverbs 3:5,6 and James 1:5, and relies on a principle that God is hiding His will from us, rather than revealing Himself to us and holding back nothing from the children He loves. This demeans Scripture, since it requires a Christian to reject the Bible as the ultimate source of authority so as to wait for a new revelation. It sets a dangerous precedent of placing our feelings and experiences above that of God's inspired Word, and therefore is akin to heresy.

We evangelicals get up in arms when a cult claims they cannot accept a blood transfusion because the Old Testament warns against "eating blood," or when an obscure passage is relied upon to defend the cultic practice of baptizing for the dead, but we don't bat an eye when someone in our own camp speaks in a way that places personal experience over God's revealed Word. This kind of theology, in my view, rejects the depiction of God in the New Testament as loving and caring, and replaces it with the remote and mysterious god of the pagans. He reduced to the level of a genie.

The apostle John, in his first epistle, marveled at the love of God: "How great is the love the Father has lavished on us, that we should be called the children of God! And that is what we are!" (1 John 3:1). It would have been great to be God's neighbor, and an honor to be His friend, but God has done immeasurably more than that. He has made us His children, causing John to exult in the wonder of it all. Later in that same book John tells us that "God is love." Love is the very essence of His character. To do anything unloving is not Godlike. How could a loving Father, One who cares so much for us that He adopted us as His sons and daughters, hide His will from us? When He sent His son, Christ didn't hide. Jesus went about performing miracles, healing the sick, teaching the multitudes, and ministering to everyone in need. If we are to believe in a secretive God, He would have sent a Savior that hid in the wilds, daring people to come look for Him.

One significant difference between Christianity and every other religion is that there is absolutely nothing to hide in Christianity. There are no secret hand signals or special words. You are not told the secrets of true spirituality when you reach a certain level, or give a certain amount of money, or attain a specific age. Anyone who walks into a Christian church today is able to find out the whole of the Gospel: God created all things; humanity sinned and is separated from God; Christ died to pay the penalty for our sins and make peace between God and people; each man or woman must choose to follow Christ completely or be separated from Him for eternity.

Of course, Christianity requires much of the believer—they must give to God their entire life, to let Him use it and shape it as He sees fit. He wants you to conform to the image of His Son, Jesus Christ. It takes faith to be a Christian, but there aren't any secrets to it. Pick up any Bible and you can read the whole story. Ours is a relationship with a loving God, and it is entirely out in the open.

With that in mind, does it make sense that God would keep His will a secret from those He loves, from those He is counting on to lead others to Himself? God's longings,

His desires and pleasures, are all clear in Scripture. A sampling of verses about the will of God make it clear:

> It is God's will that you should be sanctified: that you should avoid sexual immorality; that each of you should learn to control his own body in a way that is holy and honorable (1 Thessalonians 4:3,4).

> Be very careful, then, how you live—not as unwise but as wise, making the most of every opportunity, because the days are evil. Therefore do not be foolish, but understand what the Lord's will is. Do not get drunk on wine, which leads to debauchery. Instead, be filled with the Spirit (Ephesians 5:15-18).

> Epaphras, who is one of you and a servant of Christ Jesus, sends greetings. He is always wrestling in prayer for you, that you may stand firm in all the will of God, mature and fully assured (Colossians 4:12).

> Be joyful always; pray continually; give thanks in all circumstances, for this is God's will for you in Christ Jesus (1 Thessalonians 5:16-18).

> Submit yourselves for the Lord's sake to every authority instituted among men: whether to the king, as the supreme authority, or to governors, who are sent by him to punish those who do wrong and to commend those who do right. For it is God's will that by doing good you should silence the ignorant talk of foolish men (1 Peter 2:13-15).

You see, God's will is that you be holy, wise, mature, joyful, prayerful, and submissive. Doesn't that describe the person who remains close to God's heart? The person who truly knows the Lord develops a love for Him and a closeness to Him, so that He begins to shape one's character and values. Soon He is filling up your thoughts with His thoughts, so that you have the mind of Christ and live according to His will. There isn't any secret to that. He wants you to love Him. When you love God you live in His will.

Paul, in that famous passage in Romans 12, speaks of God's will in this character-shaping context when he says, "I urge you, brothers, in view of God's mercy, to offer your bodies as living sacrifices, holy and pleasing to God—this is your spiritual act of worship. Do not conform any longer to the pattern of this world, but be transformed by the renewing of your mind. Then you will be able to test and approve what God's will is—his good, pleasing, and perfect will" (Romans 12:1,2). One does not divine God's will. One lives God's will as one comes to know Him through His Word.

This concept of growing close to God so that you can live out His will, or live to please Him, is consistent throughout the New Testament:

> Slaves, obey your earthly masters with respect and fear, and with sincerity of heart, just as you would obey Christ. Obey them not only to win their favor when their eye is on you, but like slaves of Christ, doing the will of God from your heart (Ephesians 6:5,6).

> You need to persevere so that when you have done the will of God, you will receive what he has promised (Hebrews 10:36).

> May the peace of God, who through the blood of the eternal covenant brought back from the dead our Lord Jesus, that great Shepherd of the sheep, equip you with everything good for doing his will, and may he work in us what is pleasing to him, through Jesus Christ, to whom be glory for ever and ever. Amen (Hebrews 13:20,21).

> The world and its desires pass away, but the man who does the will of God lives forever (1 John 2:17).

The will of God is something that you do, something that you live out as you abide in Him. You must read His Word if you are to gain His mind. This doesn't mean that you open your Bible and point to a verse, hoping it will reveal your course of action as if it were Aladdin's lamp. Instead, it means you get into a pattern of regularly reading God's thoughts as expressed in the Bible, so that you are exposed to their life-changing power.

## Pray As You Read

Paul prayed for believers in Colosse:

> For this reason, since the day we heard about you, we have not stopped praying for you and asking God to fill you with the knowledge of his will through all spiritual wisdom and understanding. And we pray this in order that you may live a life worthy of the Lord and may please him in every way: bearing fruit in every good work, growing in the knowledge of God, being strengthened with all power according to his glorious might so that you may have great endurance and patience, and joyfully giving thanks to the Father, who has qualified you to share in the inheritance of the saints in the kingdom of light. For he has rescued us from the dominion of darkness and brought us into the kingdom of the Son he loves, in whom we have redemption, the forgiveness of sins (Colossians 1:9-14).

If you want to know the mind of God, pray through His Word. Pray as you read that God would enlighten your heart and mind, so that you may know Him.

When I came to Regent College I was asked to teach a hermeneutics course, so I went to the library to find the best books on interpreting Scripture. I looked through all the books written on that topic during the past decade, the 1980s, and read about ten of them carefully. They all said the same thing: Read the Bible as you would any other book. I was astounded. No one mentioned the importance of praying through Scripture. The role of the Holy Spirit seemed to be driven out by academic scholarship. The Word of God is different; it is unique. We cannot fully understand His Word without the enablement of the Spirit. Reading the Bible as a scholarly or intellectual exercise is certainly possible, but to receive the full blessing of the Lord's Word, and to understand His full meaning, we must approach the Scriptures through the Spirit of God.

I used to read the Bible for its academic merit, and I will confess I got little spiritual benefit from it. God didn't speak to me; it didn't change my heart. Then I read about a scholar who found his Bible study dry until he asked God for enlightenment. He began praying, "Lord, speak to me through Your Word." He did not simply want to read the stories; he wanted to know God's heart. At first he noticed very little difference in his reading. But soon, within three weeks of praying that prayer as he read, his heart began to burn within him. God began revealing to him how His Word should change his life. He developed a love for His teaching. God heard his prayer and began to speak to him through His Word. When I worked on translating the book of Proverbs for the NIV, I spent 60 hours a week on that text. But after 10 weeks of work, I was farther away from God than when I began because I forgot to pray that scholar's prayer.

Paul recognized the need for the Holy Spirit and prayer in reading God's Word. He knew that the people of Colosse needed a vibrant experience with Scripture if they were to be filled with all spiritual wisdom and understanding. And he knew that the result of meeting God in this way would be spiritual maturity.

Before you begin to read your Bible, pray for the Lord to speak directly to you through His Word. Pray that the Holy Spirit will enlighten you. Having spiritual understanding is nothing mystical; it means having God's Spirit teach you. Prayer can never be separated from reading God's Word.

## Memorize and Meditate

If we are really to know God's Word, not only will we want to read it, but also we should memorize it and meditate on it. That way the Word of God can speak to us, counsel us, and guide us. Usually when I am faced with a major decision, my training in Scripture comes to the fore, enabling me to think through what the Bible says about the issue at hand. It is possible to create a reservoir of God's wisdom, and to have it with you at all times. In the words of the psalmist, "Blessed is the man who does not walk in the counsel of the wicked or stand in the way of sinners or sit in the seat of mockers. But his delight is in the law of the LORD, and on his law he meditates day and night. He is like a tree planted by streams of water, which yields fruit in season and whose leaf does not wither. Whatever he does prospers" (Psalm 1:1-3).

Some Christians want to hear the voice of God speaking to them, but I'm telling you that He is already there and He has spoken. King Solomon, the wisest man apart from Jesus who ever walked this earth, encourages us to study God's wisdom in Proverbs: "Bind them upon your heart forever; fasten them around your neck. When you walk, they will guide you; when you sleep, they will watch over you; when you awake, they will speak to you" (Proverbs 6:21,22). God will talk to you through Scriptures you have memorized.

I remember learning to ride a bike as a young boy and fearing trees. It seems that I would focus all my attention on the tree in front of me, and I would hit it every time. It occurred to me that to avoid hitting the tree I had to look elsewhere, so I began to focus my attention on where I should be going rather than the obstacles in my way. In the same way, I have learned in my spiritual life not to focus on temptation or I'll get hit by it every time. Instead, I have learned to look to Jesus, who saves me from the temptations as I focus on His Word.

I know of a student who came to a professor with a besetting sin. He had tried to stop thinking about this particular sin, but it seems the more he tried not to, the more Satan brought temptation before him. So the professor sat down with this young man and wrote out a series of Bible verses that spoke directly to his sin. He put them on a three-by-five card so the student could carry it with him wherever he went. Anytime he found himself in a situation where he was tempted to sin, he was to pull out that card and read the appropriate Scripture. He soon had those verses memorized, and he found victory because he was able to strengthen his mind with the thoughts of God.

That is the same principle Jesus used in Matthew 4, when He was tempted by Satan. The devil came to Jesus, who had been fasting for 40 days, and said, "Take the shortcut. Turn these stones into bread. If you are really God, you should be able to do it." The temptation was to step out of the constraints the Holy Spirit had put in Christ's heart and to take matters into His own hands. It was the Spirit who had led Christ into the wilderness. Would Jesus act independently of the Father to satisfy His hunger? But the Lord fought back with Scripture from Deuteronomy 8:3: "Man does not live on bread alone but on every word the comes from the mouth of the LORD." It is better to obey God than to satisfy human desires.

So Satan came back with a second temptation, this time that of testing God's character. He encouraged Jesus to leap from the top of the temple, ostensibly to test if God would save Him, though perhaps also to make a public spectacle of His messiahship. Again, Christ fought with Scripture, again from Deuteronomy: "It is also written: Do not put the Lord your God to the test." Jesus was not going to test God's character to accommodate the desire of the masses.

Finally, Satan offered the toughest temptation of all: a smooth path to power. He showed Christ the wealth of the world and said, "All this I will give you if you will bow down and worship me." Think of it: Satan offered to Jesus everything that the heavenly Father said He would have, but without having to die on the cross. But Jesus, seeing how this would deny God His rightful worship, one more time responded with God's truth from Deuteronomy: "Worship the Lord your God, and serve him only." Each time Satan came with a temptation, Jesus struck back with Scripture. You can use the same method to gain victory over temptation in your life.

God's Word has the power to defeat Satan. "The word of God is living and active. Sharper than any double-edged sword, it penetrates even to dividing soul and spirit, joints and marrow; it judges the thoughts and attitudes of the heart. Nothing in all creation is hidden from God's sight. Everything is uncovered and laid bare before the eyes of him to whom we must give an account" (Hebrews 4:12,13). Paul, in describing the method of spiritual warfare in Ephesians chapter 6, lists "the sword of the Spirit, which is the word of God" as the only offensive weapon. Do you want to begin seeing victory in your life?

Memorize appropriate Scripture so that you can defeat the evil one.

Meditation is the flip side of memorizing. You don't simply remember the words; you consider their meaning. In our culture the word "meditation" has been captured by the enemy, so that if you speak of meditation to most people they immediately conjure up an image of some Far East mystic, burning incense and wearing a sarong. It's too bad we have allowed that word to become a pejorative in the minds of many, because the Bible clearly calls us to meditate: "Do not let this Book of the Law depart from your mouth; meditate on it day and night, so that you may be careful to do everything written in it. Then you will be prosperous and successful" (Joshua 1:8).

The psalmist understood the value of meditation: "Let me understand the teaching of your precepts; then I will meditate on your wonders. . . . Oh, how I love your law! I meditate on it all day long" (Psalm 119:27,97). To meditate is simply to think on God, to focus your personal attention on the Word in an attitude of dependence on the help of God. Meditaiton is nothing to be afraid of.

If you have never meditated, simply take some time away from your busy life to sit with God in a quiet place. Unplug the phone, make sure that no one will interrupt you, and sit down with the Lord. Close your eyes and ask the Lord to help you become aware of any sin in your life, then repent of the sin and ask the Lord to forgive you. Next, ask the Lord to protect your thoughts from the enemy, and to help you use this time to fill your mind with His thoughts. Then read a portion of Scripture, and sit quietly. So much of our Christian life is talking—we talk to God in prayer, the preacher talks to us, we talk to other Christians . . . but rarely do we listen.

I believe that's why meditation is difficult for many people. It requires them to sit and listen to what God has to say, and that can be uncomfortable. Simply read a passage from God's Word, then close your eyes and reflect upon what you have read. I encourage you to write your thoughts down, to keep you focused and to keep a record of your thoughts. Some people find themselves writing messages to God, or receiving a message from Him. I am not a mystic, and I do not place this sort of thing on par with Scripture, but this is a way for me to keep in touch with the thoughts of God. Sometimes my heart burns within me and I have no doubt that God is speaking to me.

Meditation is actually a form of praying, the flip side of prayer. It is a chance to listen to the voice of the Lord as He speaks. I don't hear an audible voice, but I find that the Lord is able to fill my mind with His thoughts. This isn't a form of inspiration, but illumination. Sometimes it might last five minutes, while at other times it may go for an hour. But either way is a chance for me to stop talking and listen to God.

The most common concern about meditation is "What if Satan confuses my mind?" But I realize that the Lord is not going to speak to me about anything that is evil or opposed to the counsel of Scripture, so I trust that the illumination God offers will be valuable and deepening to my spiritual life. He uses it to help me know His Word better.

One of our students at Regent was arrested in a Muslim nation for sharing his faith. He spent 16 months in solitary confinement, a time that would have broken many men. But he used that time to meditate on God's Word, and instead of falling apart, he found his life coming together. He realized that God had a definite plan for his life, and he began to recognize his utter dependence upon the Lord.

That young man learned that God is faithful, even in the midst of hardship. His opportunity to meditate on God changed his life.

> I remembered you, O God, and I groaned;
> I mused, and my spirit grew faint.
> You kept my eyes from closing; I was too troubled
>     to speak.
> I thought about the former days, the years of
>     long ago;
> I remembered my songs in the night.
> My heart mused and my spirit inquired:
> "Will the Lord reject forever?
> Will he never show his favor again?
> Has his unfailing love vanished forever?
> Has his promise failed for all time?
> Has God forgotten to be merciful?
> Has he in anger withheld his compassion?"
> Then I thought, "To this I will appeal: the years of
>     the right hand of the Most High."
> I will remember the deeds of the LORD;
>     yes, I will remember your miracles of long ago.
> I will meditate on all your works and consider all
>     your mighty deeds. (Psalm 77:3-12).

Even Erasmus, no friend of the Reformers, confessed: "I can testify to it from experience that the scriptures are of little value when read cursorily or carelessly. But when read diligently and attentively it has such efficacy as can be found in no other book."

## Humbly Obey

It is important that we not only hear God's Word, but also obey it. Otherwise we will be deluded through His Word. Remember the story of King Balak, who sought

Balaam to curse Israel. Balaam inquired of the Lord, who told him not to go, but Balaam, greedy for both the huge sum of money and the prestige of the position, would not accept God's answer. He came back to the Lord again, asking once more if he could go to Balak. This time God said, "Go ahead," but Balaam was under God's judgment. If you are not willing to obey Him, He may allow you to hear what you want to hear.

It is a profound insight that if we want God to change His mind about what is clear in Scripture, He will appear to change His mind, but we will be under judgment. This is evident also in the story of Micaiah ben Imlah, in 1 Kings 22. The king wondered if he should go to war, so he sought the counsel of the false prophets, who encouraged him to do battle. Then the king asked Micaiah, who encouraged the king to go to war because that was what the king's messenger had told him to say. But King Ahab insisted on the truth, and Micaiah said, "You really want the truth? That's different. I saw all Israel slain." If you don't want the truth in Scripture, you won't get it. You must come to God with an honest heart, ready to obey Him. When people "refuse to love the truth and so be saved, . . . God sends them a powerful delusion so that they will believe the lie" (see 2 Thessalonians 1:10,11).

I once introduced a famous colleague who was giving a speech entitled "The Most Beautiful Woman I Know." We had all assumed the man was going to speak metaphorically about something beautiful, but instead he told us of this beautiful woman who attended his church. She had an inner radiance that just seemed to light up a room when she entered. One day my friend got up the courage to ask her how she became so beautiful. Her response was, "Grace. Every day I take time to focus on grace." Then she explained that she used the word "grace" as an acronym for her prayer time.

*G is for Gratitude.* She began each day praising God for His many blessings.

*R is for Reading* God's Word. She spent time each day learning from the Lord.

*A is Appropriating.* After reading the mind of God, she sought ways to appropriate it into her life.

*C is for Charity.* Since Christians will be known by their love, she looked for ways to help others.

*E is for Expectation.* This woman fully expected God to work through her.

Spending time in prayer and reading God's Word, and then seeking an outlet for using what you have learned will lead you to the mind of God, and will cause the Lord to work through you. Coming to Him with an expectant heart, ready to be used by God, allows Him to shape your life and character. But it first requires an attitude that you will come to Scripture ready and willing to learn what the Lord wants to teach you.

In our culture we have a debate going on, even in many churches, regarding the acceptance of homosexuality. Now this argument is biblically transparent. In both the Old and New Testaments homosexuality is clearly condemned; one must suppress the truth to not see it. But some people do not see it because they do not want to hear the truth, so God allows them to be deluded.

God not only expects us to read and memorize His Word, but He also expects us to put it into practice. In our culture we consider someone uneducated to be foolish, but the Hebrew concept of a fool was not an ignorant individual, but a person who had the truth but simply did nothing with it. As James put it, "Do not merely listen to the word, and so deceive yourselves. Do what it says. Anyone who listens to the word but does not do what it says is like a man who looks at his face in a mirror and, after looking at himself, goes away and immediately forgets what he looks like. But the man who looks intently into the perfect law that gives freedom, and continues to do this, not forgetting what he has heard but doing it—he will be blessed in what he does" (James 1:22-25). The brother of our Lord is saying that only a fool gets up in the morning, checks himself in the mirror, sees that he badly needs a wash and a shave, then walks away from the mirror and forgets all about washing and shaving.

The wise man reads Scripture, meditates on it, memorizes it, and puts it into practice. That's what God desires from each of us. He wants us exposed to His thoughts and to be thinking His thoughts, so that He can change us. That's why Paul tells us, "Finally, brothers [and sisters], whatever is true, whatever is noble, whatever is right, whatever is pure, whatever is lovely, whatever is admirable—if anything is excellent or praiseworthy—think about such things. Whatever you have learned or received or heard from me, or seen in me—put it into practice. And the God of peace will be with you" (Philippians 4:8,9).

# DEVELOP A
# HEART FOR GOD

*Delight yourself in the Lord, and He will give you the desires of your heart.*

CHAPTER FIVE

ONE WAY I KNOW God's will is by the desires of my heart. The Holy Spirit puts my desires into me, so I am convinced that I am pleasing God by doing what He would have me do.

So often it seems that Christians are not sure what they should do in a particular situation, or they become flustered waiting for God to "give them a sign," when all they really need to consider is the desire of their heart. You see, if you are walking close to the Lord, and He shapes your character and influences your life, then He also is shaping your desires. That's why David could say, "Is not my house right with God? Has he not made with me an everlasting covenant, arranged and secured in every part? Will he not bring to fruition my salvation *and grant me my every desire?*" (2 Samuel 23:5).

This does not mean that God is a genie, granting you magic wishes whenever you come before Him, but that He shapes your heart after He has cleansed it of all sin, so that your desires correspond to His. When God is in control of your life, He is also in control of your desires. The things you long for in your heart are put there by the Holy Spirit. That's why the psalmist writes, "Delight yourself in the Lord and He will give you the desires of your heart" (Psalm 37:4).

## Godly Desires

Unfortunately, many Christians seem to live under the delusion that it is a sin to follow their desires. A student once said to me, "I feel guilty if I do what I want to do!" Apparently he believed in some other God, a God who does not want to fulfill the desires of His children. As you develop a heart for God, you find that your desires change and become consonant with the heart of God.

You can find examples of this throughout Scripture. The apostle Paul regularly speaks of his desires. He tells the Romans, "*I long to see* you so that I may impart to you some spiritual gift to make you strong" (Romans 1:11). He encourages the Corinthian believers to follow their hearts: "If some unbeliever invites you to a meal *and you want to* go, eat whatever is put before you without raising questions of conscience" (1 Corinthians 10:27). He even shares why he made certain career choices when he reveals, "*it has always been my ambition* to preach the gospel where Christ was not known, so that I would not be building on someone else's foundation" (Romans 15:20). Paul simply says, "This is what I wanted to do, so I did it." There is a very legitimate place for the desires of your heart revealing the will of God. We go to Scripture first, as God's Word is the ultimate authority for the faith and practice of the Christian life, but the next most important aspect of God's guidance is to follow the desires of your heart.

This concept is a bit of an abstraction for many people. When Christ was asked to reveal the most important commandment, He said to "love the your God with all your heart and with all your soul and with all your mind. This is the first and greatest commandment. And the second is like it: Love your neighbor as yourself. All the Law and the Prophets hang on these two commandments" (Matthew 22:37-40).

But loving God can be a rather vague notion, and we need to have some sort of specific guidelines to follow. This was true of Israel, so God gave Moses the Ten Commandments as a means of guiding daily life. Calvin laid down the sound principle that the ten commandments should be read to their maximum breadth. For example, "You shall not kill" entails not to commit suicide and to eat right so that you don't kill yourself. God supplemented the ten commandments (Exodus 20) with the Book of the covenant (Exodus 24:7). This book (Exodus 21–23) gives detailed descriptions of how to put the ten commandments into practice. He further elaborated upon them in Deuteronomy. All of those details about life and worship were important, but keep in mind that God does not see the same way people see. "Man looks at the outward appearance, but the LORD looks at the heart" (1 Samuel 16:7). The central truth is that *God is looking for people who have a heart for Him.* There really is nothing abstract about it: God wants you to love Him. If you do, He will change your life.

If this is a new concept for you, think of asking a two-year-old to give thanks at the dinner table. She will begin mumbling words you may not understand, then start thanking God for the house, the dog, the table, the forks, the plates, and her toys. Eventually, just as you're beginning to wonder if you will ever eat anything that's still hot, she thanks God for the food. You see, "food" is an abstraction to her. She is thankful for the ham and the Jell-O, but the general concept of "food" is a bit harder to grasp. So it is with some Christians. They are willing to try to follow a specific pattern of behavior their pastor draws out for them, but the abstract concept of "loving God" is harder to grasp. Consequently, they are leery of someone telling them to, in the words of Calvin, "love God and do what you please." They would prefer that someone tell them exactly what to do. That's why they resort to divination to seek God's will.

That, however, is an immature way of living in Christ. If you will spend time with Him in His Word and if you will talk with Him in prayer each day, you will soon develop what Paul calls "the mind Christ." As you learn to love Him, He will conform the desires of your heart to match His desires. Then there will no longer be a question of seeking His will so much as a desire to please Him.

There are a few things to keep in mind as you ponder the desires of your heart.

### Correlated to Scripture

Your desires should come out of your time with God. That way you can be sure of following godly desires and not simply personal lusts. This means you need to develop a godly mind by spending time getting to know Him. King Solomon said to his son:

> If you accept my words and store up my commands
>   within you,
> Turning your ear to wisdom and applying your
>   heart to understanding,
> And if you call out for insight and cry aloud for
>   understanding,

And if you look for it as for silver and search for it
    as for hidden treasure,
Then you will understand the fear of the LORD
And find the knowledge of God (Proverbs 2:1-5).

Each of us must take the time to know God. Perhaps that is the biggest roadblock to maturity. We live in a hurry-up world, with fast food, instant entertainment, and information in a flash from anywhere in the world. Every technological breakthrough seems to push us toward something faster—computers calculate faster, appliances work faster, even the way we prepare our meals has gotten faster. We have come to expect everything instantly, but God is not willing to offer us instant maturity. God is a personal God, so He requires a personal relationship with you, and relationships are not instant.

If you are married, think of the day you first met your spouse. Maybe you were initially attracted, and your desire was to be with him or her. Right away you found ways in which the two of you were similar, but that didn't make you "one." Your relationship had to grow and develop over time, and the longer you stayed in it, the more it changed you. When you were first married, you found yourself making adjustments to please your partner, and it changed the way you thought about yourself and the way you thought about others. The relationship continued to grow, and eventually you noticed that your life was much different from what it had been before.

So it is with God. Because He is personal, your relationship with Him is not instant. While there may been an instant attraction (or, conversely, you may have come kicking and screaming into the relationship), it takes time to develop a close bond. The closer you are to Him, the more like Him you become.

When I first met the woman who would become my wife, I liked her, but I did not love her with all my heart, soul, mind, and strength. After these years of living with her, I love her more deeply than ever before. I love her with my whole heart. When I first met the Lord, I loved Him and I appreciated what He had done for me. Now, after decades of living with Him, I know Him better and I love Him more completely. He wants us to love Him with all our heart, soul, mind, and strength, and He wants us to love our neighbors as ourselves.

The heart that loves God completely can be trusted to have godly desires. When you really love God and your neighbor, you can be very comfortable following your heart's desires because they are not self-ambitious and self-centered. Jesus said in Matthew 7:12, "In everything do to others what you would have them do to you, for this sums up the Law and the Prophets." Within the framework of loving God and your fellow man, you are free to follow the desires of your heart.

### Correlated to Submission

Paul reminds us in Romans 12:1 to offer our bodies as "living sacrifices, holy and pleasing to God." He calls us to give our entire lives to the Lord, and he goes on to say that this action will change us: "Do not conform any longer to the pattern of this world, but be transformed by the renewing of your mind" (verse 2a). As you spend time with God, His thoughts transform your thoughts and your mind is made new. It is clean; it thinks in a completely new way; it seeks the same things that God seeks. That transforms your life. So, Paul adds, "Then you will be able to test and approve what God's will is—his good, pleasing, and perfect will" (verse 2b). As you are committed to Him, and as you follow your heart's desire, you will approve God's perfect will.

If you have always wanted to feel as though you were right with God, and in the center of His will, you need to present your body to Him as a living sacrifice. That is, you need to give God your entire life. I know many Christians who seem to want to offer God pieces of their lives. They give God some of their time, some of their attention, and some of their heart. But He isn't interested in people who go only halfway.

As a matter of fact, Christ's message to the wealthy church of Laodicea is that they had better decide if they are with Him or against Him, because He is going to spit out those who are lukewarm. He says this because He cares for these people, and He points out that "those whom I love I rebuke and discipline" (Revelation 3:19). The Lord is calling us to offer Him the totality of our lives—all of our activities, all of our attitudes, even our very bodies. He wants us to offer them completely to God.

Note that our bodies are "living sacrifices" to Him, in contrast to the dead sacrifices of the Old Testament. We are alive, we have made a choice, and we are ready to be used by God as we follow His program of guidance. When a Christian (who according to the Bible is a priest) offers his total life as a sacrifice to God it is a sacred service, an act of worship.

Such an act represents a complete change in the life of the individual. He or she will no longer be like the rest of the world, living according to the lifestyle of this present evil age, but will be transformed, literally "metamorphosed" from the inside out. The key to this change is that God completely renews the mind. Thoughts, attitudes, feelings and actions are different because of the influence of God. And as you continue seeking spiritual input

85

through God's Word and prayer, He keeps changing your life.

The result of all this is that you will come to approve and desire God's will rather than your own will for your life. Further, you will find that God's will is what is good for you: It is complete, and it pleases God in every way. It is all you need. However, it is only by presenting your body as a living sacrifice that the Lord can renew your mind and allow you to understand and enjoy the will of God.

Consider the life of Jesus Christ. He offered Himself totally to the Father, to be used to fulfill God's holy plan. He was asked to literally present His body as a sacrifice. We talk about offering our bodies to the Father in some metaphorical way, but Christ knew that He was actually going to suffer and die if He obeyed His Father. The divine part of Jesus wanted to go through with it, but the human part of Him struggled. "Father, if you are willing," He prayed in the Garden of Gethsemane, "take this cup from me." He knew the agony of becoming sin itself and being separated from His loving Father. He knew the physical pain that lay before Him over the next 24 hours. Still, He concluded, "Yet not my will, but yours be done" (Luke 22:42). In the end, Christ was willing to obey, even though He knew the great cost involved. He was willing to confirm God's will, which called Christ to present His body as a sacrifice. In doing so He set an example that we all can follow.

### Correlated to Faith

Does your heart tell you this is the right thing to do? Whatever you can't do in faith, you ought not do at all. You must be able to do it with a hearty "Amen," or you have to ask yourself if this is truly the action God would have you take.

Paul follows his exhortation to present our bodies as living sacrifices in Romans 12:1,2 with the reminder to "think of yourself with sober judgment, in accordance with the measure of faith God has given you" (verse 3). That is, think carefully about your faith and trust in God. Faith is the power given by God to each saint to fulfill his or her ministry. It can be highly subjective, but the idea is that your faith will be able to believe in that which you are doing. If your heart says it is not right, then you should stop doing it. "Everything that does not come from faith is sin," Paul says in Romans 14:23. If your heart is condemning you, it is sinful. You must have a free conscience in what you are choosing to do.

I once had a long talk with a woman at our church about the issue of alcohol. She was convinced it was sinful for her to drink any alcohol, and therefore made the assumption that it was wrong for *any* Christian to partake of alcohol. "But didn't Christ turn the water into wine at the wedding of Cana?" I asked, playing the devil's advocate. "And didn't the Lord drink wine at the last supper?"

"Nonsense," she told me. "Wine back then was only as potent as grape juice."

"Really? Then why does Paul warn us not to be drunk with wine?"

Disgusted with my attitude, the woman turned away and proceeded to tell everyone of my "heresy".

The issue of alcohol seems as good a place as any to discuss the matter of faith. The Scriptures say much about the dangers of drinking wine, but clearly the issue of drinking wine is not spiritually wrong for everyone. If Christ could not only drink wine, but also make it part of the sacraments, then surely one could draw the conclusion that a Christian may drink wine as long as he or she does not get drunk.

However, some people are not free in their spirit to imbibe. They feel it is improper (perhaps for a good reason) for them to take a drink, and no one should argue with them about it. The Scriptures call us to accept those who cannot drink "without passing judgment on disputable matters. One man's faith allows him to eat everything, but another man, whose faith is weak, eats only vegetables. The man who eats everything must not look down on him who does not, and man who does not eat everything must not condemn the man who does, for God has accepted him. Who are you to judge someone else's servant? To his own master he stands or falls" (Romans 14:1-4).

We are called to accept others, and warned never to flaunt our freedom. "If anyone regards something as unclean, then for him it is unclean," Paul says in Romans 14:14. If you feel in your spirit that you cannot become involved in an activity, then for heaven's sake do not participate. It would be wrong for you to do so. Part of having a heart for God and following His will is discerning what your own heart is telling you. Do your desires correlate with your faith? Then go ahead. If not, then do not go forward. And remember, "The kingdom of God is not a matter of eating and drinking, but of righteousness, peace, and joy in the Holy Spirit" (Romans 14:17).

A good case can be made for not drinking, as in Proverbs 23:

> Listen my son, and be wise, and keep your heart
>     on the right path.
> Do not join those who drink too much wine . . . .
> Who has woe? Who has sorrow? Who has strife?
>     Who has complaints?

Who has needless bruises? Who has bloodshot
    eyes?
Those who linger over wine, who go to sample
    bowls of mixed wine.
Do not gaze at wine when it is red, when it sparkles
    in the cup, when it goes down smoothly.
In the end it bites like a snake and poisons like a
    viper (verses 19,20,29-32).

As God's people we need to offer the world a good testimony, which means never allowing alcohol to control our lives. But God's Word also celebrates the joy of drinking wine in Judges 9:13, so the point is that each of us must allow the Holy Spirit to rule our choices.

Keep in mind that each of us is unique in the eyes of God. We all have different desires, unique motivations and longings. The important thing to keep in mind is that God gave you your desires, so make sure they correlate with your faith, then move forward.

Of course, one of the difficulties of faith is learning to wait on God. Sometimes the Lord, in His sovereignty, chooses not to move immediately, even though He has said He would act. Many times in Scripture God's people have had to wait patiently. Abraham waited years to witness the birth of his son. Joseph waited for what must have seemed an eternity to be set free from an unjust situation. Hannah waited long for a son. Occasionally God calls us to wait.

It is a hard thing to wait, but it is made easier for the Christian who has faith in God. I once had to wait a long time for the Lord to answer a prayer that sprang from the desire of my heart. I learned that God's timing is perfect. We cannot always know why He chooses to act as He does, but we can be sure that, if we remain close to Him, He hears our prayers and will act on them in His perfect time.

There is nothing wrong with asking God for the desires of your heart. Sometimes, as in the case of Paul and his affliction, the Lord answers "no." In 2 Corinthians 12:7-10, Paul admits to a problem:

> To keep me from becoming conceited because of these surpassingly great revelations, there was given me a thorn in my flesh, a messenger of Satan, to torment me. Three times I pleaded with the Lord to take it away from me. But he said to me "My grace is sufficient for you, for my power is made perfect in weakness." Therefore I will boast all the more gladly about my weaknesses, so that Christ's power may rest on me. That is why, for Christ's sake, I delight in weaknesses, in insults, in hardships, in persecutions, in difficulties. For when I am weak, then I am strong.

You have got to admire a man who admits he has been denied a request from God, yet trusts God all the more. Paul understood that God allows hard things to come into the lives of Christians for a reason: He wants us to mature in Christlikeness, and we seem to mature faster and better during tough times than during easy times. The tough times taught Paul to rely on his faith in God. The Lord has a plan, a strategy behind His actions, and since God has shown Himself to be trustworthy at other times, surely He can be trusted for this also.

I have long thought that Joseph doesn't get the respect he deserves from Christians. He was an outstanding young man, who through no fault of his own had to endure suffering unjustly. Like our Lord, he learned obedience through the things he suffered. Joseph was sold by jealous brothers into slavery, unjustly accused of a crime, forced to spend many years in prison, and neglected by those whom he helped along the way. Yet the reason Joseph is such a heroic example is not because he survived difficult circumstances, but because he allowed those circumstances to draw him close to God. He learned to rely on the Lord, and God renewed his mind. He had faith in God even during the darkest days, and the Lord not only used Joseph mightily, but also gave him the desire of his heart— rapprochement with his brothers.

Don't think that a no answer from God, or the rise of difficult circumstances, means that God is necessarily displeased with you. He might just be trying to draw you closer to Himself. He may be using it as a way to build your faith.

Some members of Joseph's family may have balked at the idea of serving a pagan king like Pharaoh. But Joseph saw the Lord using the situation as a way to minister to others and fulfill His desires. Scripture doesn't say that Joseph struggled with the decision. He believed in God and the action correlated with his faith, so he went ahead.

If your heart tells you not to do something, don't do it. But if your heart is close to God and tells you your action is right, then follow the leading of your heart.

### Correlated to Prayer

If I want to remain close to my wife, if I want to really know her and have a good feeling for how our relationship is doing, I need to spend time talking with her. Anytime I get too busy to talk, and let the pressures of this life pile up while neglecting to interact with her on them, our relationship suffers. We stop communicating, and so we stop understanding each other as well. Perhaps we no longer think first of what pleases the other person, and soon we have erected a barrier between the two of us.

So it is between the Christian and God. To remain close, you must talk. When you stop talking, you stop understanding what God wants. The Christian needs to spend time in prayer so that he can remain in close communication with his heavenly Father.

This is where a proper understanding of James 1:5 comes in: "If any of you lacks wisdom, he should ask God." When we pray to God for wisdom, we are looking for Him to develop the *character* of wisdom in our lives. "The wisdom that comes from heaven is first of all pure, then peace-loving, considerate, submissive, full of mercy and good fruit, impartial and sincere" (James 3:17).

When we pray, we ask the Lord to create in us His character. Rather than asking for Him to "reveal His will," we ask Him to develop His character of wisdom in our lives. Then we will know how He thinks and what is important to Him; then we will truly know His will.

Our desires ought to move us to prayer. I am accountable for my walk with God, so I ought to be sharing my heart with Him. What moves you? Share that with the Lord. What makes you weep? Tell your Father about it. Part of God shaping the desires of our hearts is giving Him an opportunity to teach us. It is seeing how the Lord thinks about things, in order that we may gain His mind. Paul tells us to "pray in the Spirit on all occasions with all kinds of prayers and requests" (Ephesians 6:18).

The exhortation to "pray without ceasing" means that we will be in constant communication with the Lord, talking with Him about all sorts of things that come into our lives. I don't mean that you have to ask His opinion about what to have for breakfast, but that you are regularly thinking of God, talking with Him, and open to Him. Paul says in Romans 8:6 that "the mind controlled by the Spirit is life and peace," and by that I believe He means we can allow our minds to be continually under the influence of the triune God. That way you will know the mind of God because you will be thinking His thoughts.

Christians seem to be afraid of talking about the desires of the heart, for fear they will be led astray by Satan, the deceiver. But God is greater than Satan, and if God is controlling your mind, and if you are in communication with Him through Scripture and prayer, then you can trust your conscience to warn you when you begin to step out of line. You can rely on the desires of your heart, because God is in control of them.

# SEEK WISE COUNSEL

▼

*He who walks with the wise becomes wise.*

CHAPTER SIX

*G*OD HAS A PROGRAM of guidance for His children. First, and most important, He guides us through His Word. Second, as we draw close to Him, He guides us through our own godly desires. Third, He guides us through the wise counsel of others—but note that this comes *after* guidance from our own desires. You must develop a heart for God personally, not merely rely on someone else having a righteous heart.

I have had the opportunity to walk with godly men, and I have been profoundly impacted because of their influence. There is a synergy that develops when God's people are together; that's why the writer to the Hebrews encourages us to "not give up meeting together, as some are in the habit of doing, but let us encourage one another" (Hebrews 10:25). God did not just give us salvation; He also gave us the church as part of His plan for this world. The church allows the body of Christ to meet corporately for worship, to encourage one another in the faith, and to hold one another accountable for growth.

## The Burning Fire

A pastor once used the analogy of a burning fire to represent the church. He told me that if you place many logs together and strike a match, the mass of logs will ignite and create a roaring fire. As long as the logs are together, the fire continues. But if you take one burning log out of the fire, the flame will soon die out. Nothing changed in the log; it is still the same flammable material as before. But something changed in the environment; without the heat and flame of the other logs, it simply won't burn as readily. "So it is with Christians," he said to me. "As long as we are together, we burn for Christ as lights in the darkness. But if you separate one Christian away from the church, in very little time he will be reduced to a smolder."

The church is a body of believers gathered together by the Holy Spirit for the purpose of carrying out the principles of God's Word. The Lord designed the body of Christ not just to constitute a dwelling place for God, but also to have a structure for sharing His truth so that those far away from God can be brought near and those near can be built into maturity. "It was he who gave some to be apostles, some to be prophets, some to be evangelists, and some to be pastors and teachers, to prepare God's people for works of service, so that the body of Christ may be built up until we all reach unity in the faith and knowledge of the Son of God and become mature, attaining to the whole measure of the fullness of Christ" (Ephesians 4:11-13). One of the reasons God puts mature Christians into your social circle is so that you have someone to turn to for wise counsel.

## The Counsel of the Godly

Solomon had much to say about seeking counsel:

Let the wise listen and add to their learning, and let the discerning get guidance (Proverbs 1:5).
For lack of guidance a nation falls, but many advisers make victory sure (11:14).
The way of a fool seems right to him, but a wise man listens to advice (12:15).
Wisdom is found in those who take advice (13:10).
Plans fail for lack of counsel, but with many advisers they succeed (15:22).
Listen to advice and accept instruction, and in the end you will be wise (19:20).
Make plans by seeking advice; if you wage war, obtain guidance (20:18).
The pleasantness of one's friend springs from his earnest counsel (27:9).

There is a time to seek wise counsel, to listen to the mature, trusted voice of other Christians. That is particularly important in light of the direction our culture is going. We are swamped with sexual messages, inundated with brutality, and engulfed with violence. Our entertainment is filled with negative images. The average American home has the television on seven hours per day, and it brings in very little love or courtesy or consideration. Instead we are filled with news reports, dramas, and comedies that explore nothing but ruthlessness, innuendo, and bravado. There are no tender emotions on television.

The result is what has been called the "Medusa syndrome." You remember Medusa, the snake woman of Greek mythology. If you looked at her, your heart would turn to stone, for you were looking at the face of evil. In essence you became like what you saw. That's the impact most television has on our lives. We watch it, and we become like it.

Psalm 1 contrasts the tenderness of God's people with the insensitivity of those who reject God. The hardening effect of sin on our lives is evident when we read:

> Blessed is the man who does not walk in the counsel of the wicked, or stand in the way of sinners, or sit in the seat of mockers. But his delight is in the law of the LORD, and on his law he meditates day and night. He is like a tree planted by streams of water, which yields its fruit in season and whose leaf does not wither. Whatever he does prospers. Not so the wicked! They are like chaff that the wind blows away. Therefore the wicked will not stand in the judgment, nor sinners in the assembly of the righteous. For the LORD watches over the way of the righteous, but the way of the wicked will perish.

## Staying Accountable

Robert Louis Stevenson created the story of Dr. Jekyl and Mr. Hyde, in which a charming young medical doctor creates a potion that takes away all of the social graces that culture creates. Whenever Jekyl drinks the concoction, he turns into the brutish Hyde. Though frightened, the young doctor is fascinated with the life of this evil man, and continues his experiments against the counsel of wise friends. But eventually the evil takes over completely, and by the end of the story he is turned into Hyde even without having drunk the potion. That is exactly what is happening in our culture. We have become so accustomed to the pervasive evil in our world that it no longer bothers us. We have become dulled to the pain, and evil now rules the day. Alexander Pope expressed the truth this way:

Vice is a monster of frightful mien, as to be hated, needs but to be seen. But seen too oft, too familiar that face, we must first endure, then pity, then embrace.

Before the 1960's in North America, homosexuality was of frightful mien as to be hated, needed but to be seen. But the media kept it before our faces. In the 1970's we thought of it as a sickness, but now our society embraces it as a viable, alternative lifestyle.

Christian brothers and sisters can help keep us accountable to live as Christians in an unchristian world. They can ask the hard questions, offer a new perspective, and be used by God to influence our lives. We can seek their counsel when we are unclear from Scripture what God would have us do and unsure of our God-given desires.

The elders in the church of Antioch felt they were called to send someone out to preach the gospel of Christ. They came together to pray about their decision. "While they were worshipping the Lord and fasting, the Holy Spirit said, 'Set apart for me Barnabas and Saul for the work to which I have called them.' So after they had fasted and prayed, they placed their hands on them and sent them off" (Acts 13:2,3). I find this passage significant for two reasons. First, Saul, who no doubt had some idea that he was going to be preaching the good news, waited for the church leadership to confirm the decision. Second, the elders all agreed upon their representatives, so the Lord made His mind clear to everyone. That unanimity was important, since the entire church would have to send and support these missionaries.

## To Whom Do I Turn?

It is imperative that you look for a mature Christian whom you trust and admire, and that you are willing to listen to counsel even if you do not appreciate it. It has been my experience that many Christians will go to counsel for one of two reasons: Either they aren't close to the heart of God themselves, so they are looking for a backdoor into His will, or else they aren't looking as much for wise counsel as for approval from another person. But neither of those reasons honors God. The former suggests that maturity isn't important, and the latter reveals a person too weak to have his own convictions.

God wants us to first go to Him, then explore our own desires, so that we are sure we are walking closely with Him before relying on anyone else. And when we do seek counsel from another person, it should be a person in whom we have confidence of spiritual maturity. The mature person knows Scripture. Turning to an immature believer, or even a nonbeliever, is the height of folly. How will God use that person to develop your character and give you spiritual direction?

King Rehoboam serves as an example for modern Christians. His father, King Solomon, had burdened the nation of Israel with forced labor and heavy taxes to pay for his many buildings and projects. The nation became exhausted, its strength sapped. When Rehoboam became king, the people came before him and encouraged him to lighten their load: "Your father put a heavy yoke on us, but now lighten the harsh labor and the heavy yoke he put on us, and we will serve you" (1 Kings 12:4).

This could have been Rehoboam's finest hour. Had he done what the people had requested, they would have loved their king for considering their needs. Israel could once again have been a proud and powerful nation. But Rehoboam needed time to think it over. He had waited long to be king, longing for the ultimate power and glory of the crown. Now that the throne was his, the first situation he faced was a complaint from the working class. He told the people to come back in three days for his answer, and he consulted with the elders who had assisted his father, King Solomon, during his lifetime. "How would you advise me to answer these people?" he asked them.

The counselors replied, "If today you will be a servant to these people and serve them and give them a favorable answer, they will always be your servants" (verse 7). I find this a wonderfully spiritual answer. To be a good leader, the counselors tell him, you must be a servant—a very biblical perspective, and one that Christ Himself would have offered.

But Rehoboam had no intention of becoming a *servant*. He had waited all these years to be a *master*, and he was intent on ruling. So the Scriptures tell us that "Rehoboam rejected the advice the elders gave him and consulted the young men who had grown up with him and were serving him" (verse 8). In other words, the king refused to listen to experienced counsel and went instead to his yes-men for guidance.

> The young men who had grown up with him replied. "Tell these people who have said to you, 'Your father put a heavy yoke on us, but make our yoke lighter'—tell them, 'My little finger is thicker than my father's waist. My father laid on you a heavy yoke; I will make it even heavier. My father scourged you with whips; I will scourge you with scorpions'" (verses 10,11).

The young king followed the advice of these syco-phants, and ended up splitting his kingdom because of it. Had he done what his wise counselors had advised, he would have remained king over Israel.

Remember, God wants to use this process to shape your character and help you grow into maturity. It only makes sense that He will use those close to Him to share His wisdom.

## Biblical Advisers

Nearly every king mentioned in Scripture relied on advisers to share their wisdom in difficult situations. David and Solomon turned to their trusted counselors when in need. Moses spoke with his father-in-law. In the early church the believers looked to the disciples for counsel. Even Paul had those he could turn to for wisdom. First it was Barnabas, and Paul was also willing to listen to the leadership of the church. In Acts 21:20-25 the elders of the church in Jerusalem warned Paul that his life might be in danger, and in devising a plan to protect him they bluntly told him, "So do what we tell you." There probably weren't many people willing to speak to Paul that way, yet he listened to them. On the other hand, Paul knew the desires of his heart and followed them. When his friends had earlier tried to dissuade him from returning to Jerusalem, Paul said, "Why are you weeping and breaking my heart? I am ready not only to be bound, but also to die in Jerusalem for the name of the Lord Jesus" (Acts 21:13).

The apostles told all Christians to watch over each other with loving care and prayer, but they also appointed in each congregation guardians, called elders, who would look after the people as shepherds look after sheep, leading them by example away from all that is harmful and toward all that is good. By virtue of their role, the elders are called shepherds and are spoken of in terms that express leadership (1 Thessalonians 5 and Hebrews 13). The congregation, for its part, is to acknowledge the God-given authority of its leaders and follow their lead.

This pattern is already present in the Old Testament, where God is the Shepherd of Israel and kings, prophets, priests, and elders are called to act as His agents in an undershepherd role. In the New Testament, Jesus the Good Shepherd is also the Chief Shepherd and the elders are His subordinates. The apostle Peter called himself an elder under Christ. The role of the elder demands spiritual maturity and stable Christian character, as well as a well-ordered personal and family life.

Listen to your church; God placed you there for a reason. You have a pastor and church leaders in authority over you, and you need to pay attention to their counsel. A few years ago I had a student who was always changing churches—it seemed as though every other month he was telling me about the problems at his new church. "Why don't you just stay put?" I asked him one day. He proceeded to tell me about all the sin problems in each of the churches he had been at, and how he had no intention of "being part of an apostate church."

Unfortunately, the real reason this young man wouldn't stay in one church was that he did not want to be under anyone's authority. He saw himself as the Lone Ranger of the Christian church, riding off to shoot down the sinners plugging the pews of the house of God. But our Lord doesn't work that way. Every Christian is under authority, and I warned this young man that he was headed for trouble if he had no one to keep him accountable. A common denominator with all of the famous preachers who have fallen into sin in recent years is that they had no one to whom they had to listen, or at least no one to whom they would or could go.

Do not neglect the wisdom of the church. It was designed by God specifically to assist people who need wise counsel, and He uses the church as one of the tools for shaping our lives. Look to the leadership of your local church body, and to the individuals you know who walk close to God. I have often been surprised that when I went to a man for counsel, God had already been preparing his heart to speak with me. The Lord had made evident to him my situation before I had said a word. We have a mighty God who controls all things through His sovereign will, and He was looking out for me.

## What Will I Say?

In practical terms the most difficult part of seeking counsel is often broaching the subject with the adviser. We worry about looking foolish or incompetent, and that scares some people away. But you must keep in mind that God will use your situation not just to help you, but as an opportunity for someone else to minister. In other words, your request for counsel is a chance for God to work not only in your own life but in the life of the counselor as well.

That puts a whole new spin on your situation. You begin to see how God works in the larger world, not just in your life. For example, as I have spent time preparing this manuscript, the Lord has arranged for many people to talk with me about God's will for their lives. That has forced me to carefully think through the theology behind my words, and to consider the issue from various points of view. Their requests have made me a better scholar, and they were probably unaware that God was working in my life at the same time He was working in theirs. I encourage you to pray about whom you will talk with regarding your concern, so that God can prepare them as well as you.

It may seem obvious to you, but it is probably best to ask permission before stating the situation. The simple request, "May I seek your counsel on something?" politely opens the door for discussion and prepares the counselor for what is to come. Then state your case as simply as possible and ask for his or her counsel. I have had people talk to me for an hour about a situation and never actually tell me what it is they would like from me. Are they looking for wise counsel? Do they need someone to do some specific task to assist them? Or are they just looking for an encouraging word? I like to know what the other person expects, and I always make it a point to pray with them so that we will be of the same mind.

There is a great example of Christians seeking counsel in Acts 15:

> Some men came down from Judea to Antioch and were teaching the brothers, "Unless you are circumcised, according to the custom taught by Moses, you cannot be saved." This brought Paul and Barnabas into sharp dispute and debate with them. So Paul and Barnabas were appointed, along with some other believers, to go up to Jerusalem to see the apostles and elders about this question (Acts 15:1,2).

In the early days of Christianity its theology was still being formed. These believers faced a crucial decision that they knew would influence many lives: Should non-Jewish believers live out Jewish customs? Christianity had grown as the believing remnant within apostate Judaism, and under Roman law was protected as a Jewish sect. But was it really necessary to turn all those Gentile Christians into practicing Jews? If they were going to take the good news of Jesus Christ throughout the Roman Empire, would they also need to exhort new believers to live as Jews?

The church was divided, so they decided to seek counsel from a greater source. The church in Jerusalem at that time was seen as the seat of Christianity, as it were, so the Christians turned to the elders in Jerusalem.

The church sent them on their way, and as they traveled through Phoenicia and Samaria, they told how the Gentiles had been converted. This news made all the brothers very glad. When they came to Jerusalem, they were welcomed by the church and the apostles and elders, to whom they reported everything God had done through them. Then some of the believers who belonged to the party of the Pharisees stood up and said, "The Gentiles must be circumcised and required to obey the law of Moses."

The apostles and elders met to consider this question. . . . The whole assembly became silent as they listened to Barnabas and Paul telling about the miraculous signs and wonders God had done among the Gentiles through them. When they finished, James spoke up: "Brothers, listen to me. . . . It is my judgment, therefore, that we should not make it difficult for the Gentiles who are turning to God. Instead we should write to them, telling them to abstain from food polluted by idols, from sexual immorality, from the meat of strangled animals and from blood. For Moses has been preached in every city from the earliest times and is read in the synagogues on every Sabbath" (verses 3-6, 12, 13, 19-21).

The decision was agreed upon, and it set a precedent that allowed the church to grow explosively over the next few years. God's people needed counsel, so they went to mature believers and presented the issue clearly, and then God worked His will through their wise counsel.

## What Is the Call of God?

Christians like to toss around the phrase "I was called" whenever they make a decision about something important. It is important that we understand the concept of

God's "call." I define it this way: *A call is an inner desire given by the Holy Spirit, through the Word of God, and confirmed by the community of Christ.* This definition makes clear the priority that must be given God's revelation and your own conviction. First, a call rises out of your own desire, your inner conviction. As you draw close to God and He shapes your mind and will, you find yourself desiring different things. Occasionally you may feel a deep conviction that the Lord wants you to do something. That is the first phase of a "calling," but it does not by itself constitute a call.

A Christian must have his inner conviction based on God's Word. As one spends time reading and meditating on Scripture, God's mind begins to confirm or reject the calling. If it is apparently confirmed through the Bible, then it must really be affirmed by the body of Christ, which is why it is so vitally important to surround oneself with godly people. I ask every person who claims he wants to be in the ministry if mature Christians in his church have confirmed that assessment. Without the affirmation of the body, one must question the legitimacy of the call, but priority must still be given to the Word of God and the desires of the heart.

First Kings 13 tells the story of a young prophet of Judah who had been told by God to go up to Bethel, condemn the altar, and then go home. He was explicitly instructed by the Lord to not eat or drink, but to go home immediately. There were some men standing close by who observed his prophecy, saw the power of this young prophet, and raced home to tell their father about it. Their father was an old prophet, and he ordered his sons to invite the younger man to their home. When the young prophet showed up, the old prophet said, "Eat and drink," but the young man explained how God warned him not to:

> The man of God said, "I cannot turn back and go with you, nor can I eat bread or drink water with you

in this place. I have been told by the word of the LORD: 'You must not eat bread or drink water there or return by the way you came.'"

The old prophet answered, "I too am a prophet, as you are. And an angel said to me by the word of the LORD, 'Bring him back with you to your house so that he may eat bread and drink water.'" (But he was lying to him.) So the man of God returned with him and ate and drank in his house (1 Kings 13:16-19).

The old prophet deluded the younger one by lying to him about what Lord said, so the young prophet followed what a man had to say rather than obeying the direct word of the Lord. Then, in this very strange story about the importance of obeying God's word, the old prophet tells the younger:

This is what the LORD says: "You have defiled the word of the LORD and have not kept the command the LORD your God gave you. You came back and ate bread and drank water in the place where he told you not to eat and drink. Therefore you body will not be buried in the tomb of your fathers" (verses 21,22).

The end result was that the young prophet was killed by a lion on his way home—harsh discipline for not obeying God's command. The point of the story is that if God clearly tells you to do something, don't disobey just because someone tells you something different. Wise counsel should be sought when the Bible and your inner desires are not clear, but the counsel of others should never negate what you heard the Lord say to you through Scripture. God's Word takes precedence over the counsel of others.

# LOOK FOR GOD'S PROVIDENCE

▼

*God is at work in the circumstances of our lives.*

## CHAPTER 7

*T*HERE IS AN ELEMENT to life that we do not control, called "providence," and that too is God's will. *Webster's Dictionary* defines providence as the benevolent guidance of God. He is at work in the circumstances of our lives, in both small ways and large. Sometimes we refer to it as "chance," because that is sometimes the way His providence appears to us.

The Bible uses the word that way; for example, Ruth 2:3 reads literally that "Ruth chanced on the field of Boaz." Her biographer makes it clear that, while it seemed mere chance, it was the Lord who superintended her life. At the beginning of her story the Lord ended the drought in Judah and gave His people food. At the end of the story it was the Lord who opened her womb and gave her offspring. God never spoke to Ruth directly, through visions or words, but He directed the affairs of her life according to His own purposes and to her good. Nothing happens to the Christian by chance. God does not have accidents;

things happen by design. Still, the element of providence is evident throughout our lives.

King Solomon once said, "The race is not to the swift or the battle to the strong, nor does food come to the wise or wealth to the brilliant or favor to the learned; but time and chance happen to them all" (Ecclesiastes 9:11). I find that a wonderful explanation for the many fortunate things that have happened to me—those times when I did nothing but somehow still managed to receive a rich blessing from God. As Solomon says, a lot has to do with the timing of life.

For example, it makes no sense that I am a Hebrew professor. I had just finished a doctorate in Greek when my Dallas Seminary professor of Hebrew resigned in the middle of the school year. The institution couldn't find anyone qualified, so they laid their hands on me and I was christened a Hebrew instructor. (Of course I had studied Hebrew in previous years.) Some people would call it dumb luck, but I prefer to see it as the providence of God.

As a young man I was waiting for a particular girl to wake up and realize I was the man of her dreams. As I waited, Elaine happened to come along and we fell in love. I don't know what ever happened to that other woman, but Elaine and I have had more than 40 wonderful years together thanks to the providence of God. Time and chance happen to everyone.

Paul said to the church in Rome, "I do not want you to be unaware, brothers, that I planned many times to come to you (but have been prevented from doing so until now)" (Romans 1:13). This demonstrates the fourth stage of God's guidance: providence. Sometimes you want to do things, and people in the body of Christ affirm you, but for whatever reason it just is not possible. The opportunity isn't there. Remember, we first look to Scripture to make sure we are following God's truth. Then we make sure we are following our heart's desire. Then we seek the wise counsel of others. All of those are steps for which we take responsibility. But sometimes things happen over which we have no control. That's providence, and occasionally we just have to bend to its will.

## Accept the Circumstances

It is possible to have a definite purpose, feel called, and have the affirmation of other Christians, yet have circumstances prevent you from carrying out your plan. Paul spoke of this matter in 2 Corinthians 1:17, when he said of his plans, "When I planned this, did I do it lightly? Or do I make my plans in a worldly manner so that in the same breath I say, 'Yes, yes' and 'No, no'?" Paul had a definite purpose, but he was unable to complete it. Sometimes, no matter how hard we try, things just don't work out that way.

My co-writer, Dr. Chip MacGregor, is a planner. He maps things out on his calendar, sets goals, and generally tries to have a plan for what he wants to accomplish in life. But Chip will tell you that he always has to leave a margin for error. Things don't always go the way he expects. Sometimes providence won't allow him to accomplish everything he had planned. At other times the Lord grants success so exceedingly and abundantly beyond all he can ask or imagine that he has to throw out his notes and start over.

The growth of management theory in churches has helped many pastors get organized and become better equipped for coordinating their ministries. Unfortunately, it has also allowed an attitude to creep into the churches that a well-conceived plan is all that is needed for a church to succeed. But not every factor can be taken into consideration. Things won't always work the way we plan them. We cannot manipulate God to do things the way we want them.

James had a teaching for those people who believe they can totally map out their future:

> Now listen, you who say, "Today or tomorrow we will go to this or that city, spend a year there, carry on business and make money." Why, you do not even know what will happen tomorrow. What is your life? You are a mist that appears for a little while and then vanishes. Instead, you ought to say, "If it is the Lord's will, we will live and do this or that" (James 4:13-17).

There is nothing wrong with making plans; as a matter of fact Solomon suggested that a leader sit down and think carefully through all the steps before beginning a major project. But the goals we set and the plans we make are not our God. We ought to say instead, "Lord, here is what I am planning to do. I think it is the right step. I've prayed about it, read Your Word, and sought the wise counsel of others. I believe this is pleasing to You. So if you will, I plan to do this." Always leave room for things not working out quite the way you planned them

In 1952 I was attending seminary and staring headlong into an uncertain future. I had no idea what God had in store for me, and I desperately wanted some sort of security. Then it hit me: I'll join the Army! I'll be an Army chaplain, so that I can have the security of a position but still be ministering to people. Everything in my life became focused on joining the military. But my heart was condemning me, because I was acting out of fear, not faith. God in His good providence saved me from my folly. Then, days before I was to be inducted, I got a telegram. Looking back, I can see why the Lord didn't want me in the Army. I wasn't cut out for the Army; I was signing up only to find a steady job.

There are a number of examples in the New Testament where Paul testifies to the role of God's providence in his life. For example, in Acts 18:21 the apostle leaves the city of Ephesus to go back and report to his home church. As he departs, he tells the Jewish believers, "I will come back if it is God's will," which is to say, "I shall return if God arranges the circumstances." And he did return to Ephesus a short time later.

On many occasions Paul spoke of visiting other congregations. To the church at Rome he wrote, "I pray that now at last by God's will the way may be opened for me to come to you" (Romans 1:10). Paul had wanted to visit Rome, but in God's providence the door was not open for him to do so. He tried to visit Bithynia, "but the Spirit of Jesus would not allow them to" (Acts 16:7). He desired to pay another visit to Corinth, but as far as we know he never made it. Sometimes the providence of God, working through time and chance, prevents us from doing what we think we would like to do. At other times it presents us with remarkable opportunities we never expected.

You have no doubt had opportunities leap out at you when you least expected them. Sometimes God will bring a person or a situation into your life that you have not had an opportunity to prepare for, and you simply rely on the fact that your heavenly Father likes to surprise His children.

A friend of mine, a professor at a Christian college, once happened to be seated in a restaurant across from another man who prayed before starting his meal. They struck up a conversation, and it turned out the man was the president of another Christian college, in town to talk with a prospective faculty member. The Lord just seemed to arrange the meeting serendipitously, and my friend ended up moving to the institution even though he had not been looking to make a change. God just superintends our circumstances, and we sometimes must respond to time and "chance."

## God Works on Our Behalf

The good news about providence is that God cares for us. He thinks about what is best for us, sends His angels to watch over us, and superintends on our behalf. He cares for us as our loving Father: "You are all sons of God through faith in Christ Jesus" (Galatians 3:26). The apostle John says in 1 John 3:9 that the seed of God actually abides in believers, so that we really are "born again" as His children. Peter encourages us to cast all our cares onto the Father, "because he cares for you" (1 Peter 5:7).

The fatherhood of God is not unique to the New Testament. God called Israel His "firstborn son" (Exodus 4:22). Why was His firstborn son languishing as a slave in a foreign country when the Father had an inheritance to give him? Before the son received his inheritance, the Promised Land, God sealed His covenant with His Son.

If old Israel was His son, how much more the church today? We are seated in the heavenlies together with the eternal Son of God, who is the expressed image of His person. What were we doing in a foreign world ruled by Satan and enslaved by sin? He released us from our captivity, entered into a new covenant with us by the Holy Spirit (who wrote His law upon our hearts), sealed us by the Holy Spirit, and is leading us to our eternal inheritance that will never fade away.

Jesus is the full expression of what it means to be the Son of God. From now on, in a way unknown in the Old Testament, God's people would address Him as "Abba, Father."

It was the mission of Jesus Christ to make God known more fully as the Father, which is why He prayed in His high-priestly prayer, "Now Father, glorify me in your presence with the glory I had with you before the world began.

I have revealed you to those whom you gave me out of the world" (John 17:5,6).

It is impossible to approach the fatherhood of God except through the mediation of the Son, Jesus Christ. "No one comes to the Father except through me," Jesus said. But for those who have faith in Christ, we have become the loved children of God.

The Lord Jesus once said, "Are not two sparrows sold for a penny? Yet not one of them will fall to the ground apart from the will of your Father" (Matthew 10:29). I'm impressed with a God so caring that He even knows when a sparrow falls. *That* is an immense God! Christ goes on to say in the next verse that even the very hairs on your head are numbered. Our heavenly Father knows all about us. Hagar was an Egyptian slave that wronged her mistress, Sarah. But when Sarah mistreated Hagar, God met her and provided for her. She warned God "The LORD who sees me." The psalmist David beautifully describes the intimate love and care of God for His children in Psalm 139:

> O LORD, you have searched me and you know me.
> You know when I sit and when I rise;
> You perceive my thoughts from afar.
> You discern my going out and my lying down;
> You are familiar with all my ways.
> Before a word is on my tongue you know it
>     completely, O LORD.
> You hem me in—behind and before;
> You have laid your hand upon me.
> Such knowledge is too wonderful for me,
> Too lofty for me to attain.

## II

> Where can I go from your Spirit?
> Where can I flee from your presence?

If I go up to the heavens, you are there.
If I make my bed in the depths, you are there.
If I rise on the wings of the dawn,
If I settle on the far side of the sea,
Even there your hand will guide me, your right
    hand will hold me fast . . .

### III

For you created my inmost being;
You knit me together in my mother's womb.
I praise you because I am fearfully and
    wonderfully made;
Your works are wonderful, I know that full well.
My frame was not hidden from you when I
    was made in the secret place.
When I was woven together in the depths of
    the earth,
Your eyes saw my unformed body.
All the days ordained for me were written in
    your book before one of them came to be. . . .

### IV

If only you would slay the wicked, O God!
Away from me, you bloodthirsty men!
They speak of you with evil intent, your adversaries
    misuse your name. Then. . . .
Search me, O God, and know my heart;
Test me and know my anxious thoughts.
See if there is any offensive way in me,
And lead me in the way everlasting.

In the first paragraph David celebrates the fact that God knows all about him, all the time, and in every place. In the second paragraph he sings that God is always present with him, whether in heaven or in the grave. In the third paragraph he proves these truths. God, You created me; You know me inside out, and look where you made your magnum opus—in the dark watery chamber of my mother's womb. You might just as well have made me in the bowels of the earth. In the last paragraph David tells us he is celebrating God's omnipotence and omnipresence in the presence of murderers who hate him and want to kill him.

What a lovely depiction of the Father planning us, creating us, and knowing us! God is there, working on our behalf.

There are two examples in the life of Jesus that depict the care that God has for His children. The first occurs after Christ's temptation. Because Jesus had not eaten in forty days and had just come through a battle with the Devil, He needed some tender care from God. So Matthew points out that when the Devil left him, "angels came and attended him" (Matthew 4:11). When, in the Garden of Gethsemane, Jesus cried out to God in anguish, Luke reveals that "an angel from heaven appeared to him and strengthened him" (Luke 22:43). What a beautiful picture of God planning for our needs and ministering to us!

### God Chose You with a Plan

Christian, keep in mind that God planned you and created you. Ephesians 1 says that you were in His plans "before the creation of the world" (verse 4), and that He planned from the very beginning to make you "holy and blameless in his sight. In love he predestined us to be adopted as his sons through Jesus Christ, in accordance with his pleasure and will" (verse 4,5). God *chose* you as one of His own; He adopted you as His child, and then, according to verses 6-8, He lavished forgiveness, grace, wisdom, and understanding on you. He chose you not because you impressed Him, but so that He could impress the world about Himself. Paul says he chooses weak people to show His strength, foolish people to show His wisdom. As David Roper says, "We are not great stuff. God surrounds Himself with incompetence. The people God uses have rarely been great people. Nietzsche looked for a 'strong kind of man, most highly gifted in intellect and will.' God looks for misfits and milquetoasts, schmucks and schlemiels. It's not that He has to make do with a bunch of fools, He chooses them."

Paul put it this way, "Brothers, think of what you were when you were called. Not many of you were wise by human standards; not many were influential; not many were of noble birth. But God chose the foolish things of the world to shame the wise; God chose the weak things of the world to shame the strong. He chose the lowly things of this world and the despised things—and the things that are not—to nullify the things that are, so that no one may boast before him" (1 Corinthians 1:26-29).

Not only did He choose you, adopt you, forgive you, and make you holy, but He also developed a plan for your life and makes it known to you: "He made known to us the mystery of his will according to his good pleasure, which he purposed in Christ, to be put into effect when the times will have reached their fulfillment—to bring all things in heaven and on earth together under one head, even Christ" (Ephesians 1:9,10). God is working out His plan on earth through His children, and eventually the rest of the world will see that we were right: Christ is indeed King. His will for us to be His holy representatives on earth is clear.

"In him we were also chosen," Paul goes on, "having been predestined according to the plan of him who works out everything in conformity with the purpose of his will, in order that we, who were the first to hope in Christ, might be for the praise of his glory" (verses 11,12). The fact is clear: God chose us to be holy. Our lives give praise and glory to God because we are evidence of His mercy, love, and holiness. This was all part of His plan, that we should live our lives to glorify Him.

"And you were also included in Christ when you heard the word of truth, the gospel of your salvation" (verse 13). Your decision to trust Christ marked a turning point. That is when you became God's child, and moved in step with His will. "Having believed, you were marked in him with a seal, the promised Holy Spirit, who is a deposit guaranteeing our inheritance until the redemption of those who are God's possession" (verses 13,14). When you made that decision to trust Christ, God in His loving care gave you a special gift as a mark of your salvation: He put His Holy Spirit into your life as a sign that you are truly His child.

The word translated "deposit" is a fascinating Greek word. It can be used to represent a seal—God's mark on our lives that we belong to Him. It can also mean a "down payment"—the Holy Spirit is given to us as a taste of the complete holiness we will experience in God's presence at some point in the future. Or it can mean an "engagement ring." God places the Spirit in us as a promise that, at some point in the future, we will have more of Him, and spend eternity with Him. What a wonderful promise! God cares for us as a loving Father, and He superintends our circumstances for our best.

When Elaine and I were first married, I had a desire to minister in a church. We were living in Boston at the time because I was working on my doctorate at Harvard, and as the summer approached, I desired a pastoral position in a church. We prayed for two things one Sunday morning: first, that the Lord would put me into a position where I could minister, and second, that we could remain close to the university. In Monday's mail came a letter from a church close by asking me to become its pastor. God already knew our prayer, and had the answer prepared for us before we even began praying! In His providence He provided for us in a way that was totally unexpected.

We live to please Him, but sometimes time and chance prevent us from doing what our hearts tell us we would like to do. That is part of God's providence. Attribute it to the overall plan of a God who loves you; trust that He knows best.

## We Cannot Always Know Why

In the perfect world as we imagine it, we always get the answers. We always see the "big picture" and joyfully accept God's plan. But we don't live in that perfect world, and the fact is we do not always understand the providence of God. That's why the Bible tells us that "the just will live by faith." It takes faith to trust God when bad things come crashing down.

Joseph must have wondered what he had done to deserve the raw deal he got. First he is sold into slavery, then he is bought by a guy married to a woman with an overactive imagination, and then he is forgotten by the man whom he helped while in prison. Joseph is one man who must have wondered about the providence of God. But in the end the Lord worked out his circumstances for good.

During the 1980s a uniquely American brand of theology arose that deceived many people. We usually refer to it as "prosperity theology," and only an embarrassingly wealthy culture like ours could conceive it. Its tenets went something like this: God wants you to be healthy and wealthy. If you are really walking with the Lord, He will grant you good health and make your business prosper. If you are sick, you must reject the sickness and develop more faith in God. If you head into hard times, that is evidence of your unbelief in Him.

This is all utter nonsense and blatant heresy, of course, but it found a willing audience in a society that values wealth above character. Consequently it saw quick growth, but it faded out as soon as people realized that God offers no magic prescription for economic success other than that of common sense—work hard, be thrifty, and save your money. Closeness to Christ and material prosperity have very little in common.

Agur, one of the most humble men in the Old Testament, understood that lesson. He prayed that God would not give him too much money, because he couldn't handle it. If he had too much money, Agur confessed, instead of trusting God he would depend on his wealth to give him significance and security. (See Proverbs 30.) The Bible has much to say about money, and a lot of it is good. Poverty is no virtue; it separates us from friends, denies us the leisure to enjoy reading good books and edifying music, and may even separate us from God. Agur also prayed that God would not give him too little, because he could not handle that either. "I may steal," he confessed, "and blaspheme Your name." The rich man in Proverbs is not simply a person who has a lot of money (wealth can be one of God's blessings on His children) but a person who has a lot of money and trusts in it and in himself.

Here is the paradox: God's blessings can be spiritually dangerous. We can substitute the blessings for trusting God Himself. To counteract that danger, we must constantly praise God, remember how wretched and poor we are in ourselves, and give our money away to help others in need. In fact, the real test of your faith is to give your money away to the needy, so that you too must trust God.

Using the warped theology of the "name-it-and-claim-it" people, Jesus was not a spiritual man. "Foxes have holes and birds of the air have nests, but the Son of Man has no place to lay his head" (Matthew 8:20), Christ once said in describing Himself. Apparently Christ wasn't spiritual enough, or He would simply have claimed the wealth that His Father wanted Him to have. And perhaps He should have rejected the cross, since that must have happened as a result of His lack of faith. This sort of thinking is madness, of course, but that is the logical conclusion that must be drawn from the "name-it-and-claim-it" preachers. The fact is that we do not control all our circumstances. Sometimes in God's providence difficult situations will come our way, and we must simply trust in God in spite of them.

Take the life of Paul as an example. He was beaten, thrown in prison, and exposed to death again and again. "Five times I received from the Jews the forty lashes minus one. Three times I was beaten with rods, once I was stoned, three times I was shipwrecked, I spent a night and day in the open sea, I have been constantly on the move. I have been in danger from rivers, in danger from bandits, in danger from my own countrymen, in danger from Gentiles, in danger in the city, in danger in the country, in danger at sea, and in danger from false brothers. I have labored and toiled and have often gone without sleep; I have known hunger and thirst and have often gone without food; I have been cold and naked. Besides everything else, I face the daily pressure of my concern for all the churches" (2 Corinthians 11:24-28). Paul had some tough times, and he did not always know why. But he continued to trust the Lord in spite of his circumstances.

Late in life Paul, in prison in Rome for preaching the gospel, wrote to his protégé Timothy. Rather than complaining about the circumstances of his life, he recognized that he had been obedient to what God had called him to do. "The time has come for my departure," he says in 2 Timothy 4:6-8. "I have fought the good fight, I have finished the race, I have kept the faith. Now there is in store for me the crown of righteousness, which the Lord, the righteous Judge, will award to me on that day—and not only to me, but also to all who have longed for his appearing." Paul was able to see how his circumstances were being used by the Lord to accomplish His purposes. "Now I want you to know, brothers, that what has happened to me has really served to advance the gospel. As a result, it has become clear throughout the whole palace guard and to everyone else that I am in chains for Christ. Because of my chains, most of the brothers in the Lord have been encouraged to speak the word of God more courageously and fearlessly" (Philippians 1: 12-14).

Sometimes difficult things happen and we don't know why. The Old Testament character of Job was a God-fearing man who had no end of trouble come his way as a result of a test from Satan. He looked to his friends for comfort, but they only suggested the difficulties had come because of sin in Job's life. Job knew that this was not why the Lord had allowed these things to occur, and he sought the Lord for a reason. It is interesting to read the book of Job, because he never really does get an answer from God. In essence, the Lord says, "My design, both in creation and history, includes chaos that is hostile to physical and/or social life. Nevertheless, the chaos is bounded by life. You have sufficient reason to trust Me. I have so designed both that you cannot explain it or control it. Job did so, and was blessed for his obedience.

Try to keep in mind that God in His providence will allow both positive and negative experiences to come your way. They are not necessarily a measure of your spirituality, although they may very well be a wonderful opportunity to grow in the grace and knowledge of Jesus Christ. Sometimes we are at the mercy of time and chance. Peter reminds believers that "it is better, if it is God's will, to suffer for doing good than for doing evil" (1 Peter 3:17). You may do the right thing and still have circumstances go against you. All you can do is learn to accept the fact that God has never promised life will always be fair or that we deserve an explanation for everything. There will be times you believe the Word of God is leading you to do something, it becomes the desire of your heart, and other Christians encourage you to follow your heart, but providence will not allow it. Assume that God has something else planned. Learn to trust God in spite of your circumstance.

## Do Not Put Circumstances Above God's Word

God gave us the Bible so that we would have His truth and could live our lives by its light. Do not put circumstances above God's Word. Don't allow your circumstances to contradict God's Word. For example, a situation occurs in 1 Samuel chapter 24 where King Saul, who has been chasing David and trying to kill him, goes alone into a cave to relieve himself. The men guarding David say to him, "'This is the day the Lord spoke of when he said, I will give your enemy into your hands for you to deal with as you as you wish.' David crept up unnoticed and cut off a corner of Saul's robe. Afterward, David was conscience-stricken for having cut off a corner of his robe. [In David's world, cutting off the edge of the king's robe was the signal of revolution.] He said to his men, 'The LORD forbid that I should do such a thing to my master, the LORD's anointed, or lift my hand against him, for he is the anointed of the LORD.' With these words David rebuked his men and did not allow them to attack Saul. And Saul left the cave and went his way" (1 Samuel 24:4-7).

David had the opportunity to kill his enemy. The circumstances were propitious. The ruffians around David tried to convince him with an argument of circumstance: "It's perfect! It must be God's will!" So David began to follow them, and cut off a corner of the king's garment as a sign of insurrection. But then David's conscience smote him because Scriptures say you cannot touch God's anointed. Once God has anointed someone with holy oil, the Lord Himself must dispose of him. David was not to do it on his own terms. He was not to put a fortuitous circumstance above the Word of God. You can't take a bit of good timing as concrete evidence of God's will. You can't take God's providence and make it normative for every situation, or you will get into big trouble. David could have brought permanent harm to Israel by usurping the throne through violence.

A similar event happened in 1 Samuel 26, this time David and Abishai took the initiative and sneaked into Saul's camp. They found the king asleep on the ground with his spear and water jug beside him. They had both his life and death in their hands. Abishai suggested killing the king where he lay, claiming that the Lord must have allowed this circumstance to occur and they should take advantage of it. But David would not contradict the Scriptures. He would not put his circumstance ahead of God's Word, nor would he allow the situation to take precedence over what he knew in his heart to be right. It would have been easy to attribute the circumstance to God and reason that "the Lord must want me to break the

Law." But God never calls us to sin, even for a good cause. We obey the Lord and maintain our integrity, even when we are sorely tempted to use the situation for our benefit.

It might have seemed fortuitous to Jesus that, after fasting for 40 days, there were stones nearby and He had the power to turn them into bread. But that was not what Christ was called to do, and He was not willing to let His circumstances outweigh what He knew to be right.

A friend of mine had a wonderful opportunity to see the providence of God at work not long ago. His wife had a desire to purchase something that cost about 40 dollars, and he really wanted to buy it for her, but they simply couldn't afford it. It wasn't extravagant, but it just didn't fit into their budget at the time, so they decided to wait.

A few days later he was browsing through a store and saw just what his wife wanted for a bit less money. "Wow!" he thought to himself. "God must want me to buy it— otherwise He wouldn't have had it go on sale!" That sort of reasoning will get you in trouble every time. Fortunately his good sense returned before he could break out his Visa card. They had made a decision to wait, so he thought he had better hold off until talking with his wife about it. As he arrived home that night, his wife had a big surprise for him. She had promised a woman from church a ride home from The Salvation Army, and decided to walk through the store while she waited for her friend to get ready. There on the shelf in front of her was the very item she had desired, brand new, for two dollars. Someone had donated it that morning. She knew God was honoring them for using their money wisely. He worked out the situation so she could get what she wanted without breaking the bank.

That's an example of the providence of God. He loves us and sometimes superintends situations just as a special blessing to His children. You can't plan for these situations, and you must be willing to obey God's Word and the desires of your heart first, but when they happen, remember that God ministers to you in both big ways and small ways. Like any good father, He loves His children.

# DOES THIS MAKE SENSE?

▼

*God expects us to use our good judgment.*

CHAPTER 8

*G*OD GUIDES US FIRST through His Word, then through our heartfelt desires, then the wise counsel of others, and then our circumstances. At that point we must rely on our own sound judgment. It is possible to pray, read God's Word, seek counsel, and still not feel led by God. That's the time to rely on sound judgment. God gave each of us a brain, and He expects us to put it to good use.

Several times, when I have had a student in my office talking about some struggle and looking for guidance, I have asked the question, "What makes sense? In your judgment, what would be the best thing to do?" Usually the student will suggest which alternative is best, and we will judge that against Scripture. Occasionally I've had a student stare back at me blankly as though it never occurred to him to consider making up his own mind. But if we have been so uniquely created as to have high-level thinking, it only makes sense that God will use our judgment as part of His program of guidance. Don't fall into the trap of thinking that God's guidance will always be through something spectacular or unique. Often He guides us by simply letting us use our heads. The choice that makes sense is often the one God would have us do. There are numerous examples of this sort of reasoning in Scripture:

> You and your brother Jews may then do whatever seems best with the rest of the silver and gold (Ezra 7:18).
>
> We are now in your hands. Do to us whatever seems good and right to you (Joshua 9:25).
>
> "Do what seems best to you," Elkanah her husband told her (1 Samuel 1:23).
>
> The king answered, "I will do whatever seems best to you" (2 Samuel 18:4).
>
> If it seems good to you, and if it is the will of the LORD our God, let us send word far and wide to the rest of our brothers (1 Chronicles 13:2).
>
> The whole assembly then agreed to celebrate the festival seven more days (2 Chronicles 30:23).
>
> Then the apostles and elders, with the whole church, decided to choose some of their own men and send them to Antioch (Acts 15:22).
>
> Paul had decided to sail past Ephesus to avoid spending time in the province of Asia, for he was in a hurry to reach Jerusalem (Acts 20:16).

There isn't anything startling about this. God expects us to use our decision-making capabilities to make choices. Perhaps the one surprising thing to many Christians is the order of its importance.

The natural man bases every decision on logic. Since he receives no guidance from God, he must rely on his own sound judgment to make every choice. But a Christian has the Almighty God offering a program of guidance, so "sound judgment" becomes the last part of the process. A wise philosopher said, "You cannot know certainly unless you know comprehensively." Since we see life through a big hole, we can misjudge situations. Only God sees it whole and clear. Therefore, we must think within the framework of His revelation. God's Word is certain; human reason is less certain. A Christian cannot make sound judgment without relying on Scripture, a heart purified by God, the wise counsel of others, and the circumstances the Lord sends our way. Many believers try to make every decision solely on the basis of what seems expedient or logical, and that leaves God out of the process.

## Trust God in Your Logic

Often the guidance of God is in opposition to sound judgment apart from faith, and once again we must make the decision to trust His will. When Abraham was told by God to offer Isaac as a sacrifice, the order made no sense. Isaac was the only son of an old man, to whom the promise of a huge nation had been made. That promise would go unfulfilled if Isaac were to die, and Abraham must have considered the lack of logic in God's order. His heart did not want to sacrifice his own son whom he loved dearly. And had he sought counsel, his friends probably would have told him not to go ahead with it. God's command made no sense at all, but it came directly to Abraham, so he obeyed it and was blessed because of it. Logic and human reason cannot be the sole sources of guidance for Christians. We are spiritual beings, not merely intellectual. God speaks to our hearts sometimes in direct opposition to our reason. Being a Christian isn't irrational; it is very rational within the context of faith. He rewards those who diligently seek Him.

The book of Ruth tells the story of a mature woman whose husband and two sons died. She was left with her two daughters-in-law, Orpah and Ruth.

> Then Naomi said to her two daughters-in law, "Go back, each of you, to your mother's home. May the Lord show kindness to you, as you have shown to your dead and to me. May the Lord grant that each of you will find rest in the home of another husband."
>
> Then she kissed them and they wept aloud and said to her, "We will go back with you to your people." But Naomi said, "Return home, my daughters. Why would you come with me? Am I going to have any more sons, who could become your husbands? Return home, my daughters; I am too old to have another husband" (Ruth 1:8-12).

It made no sense for the younger women to go with Naomi. The practical, logical thing for them to do was to return to their families. Parents and family members could care for them, and perhaps they could marry again.

Orpah did the practical thing: She left Naomi and returned to her family. There was nothing cruel about that it simply was the most logical thing to do. But Ruth stayed with Naomi because her heart told her it was right to do so. There are times when we as Christians are called to obey God in a way that defies logic. My own experience is that the Lord often chooses a course other than the one I would choose. Perhaps that speaks to my lack of sound reasoning, but I think more likely it reveals the great wisdom of God. He chooses a path that is supernatural, that causes me to grow in character, and that is best for me.

Logic and reason are not the priorities in God's program of guidance.

Jesus said that as He took up a cross and died, so we too must take up a cross. Our cross is not giving up something we like, such as giving up candy for Lent, nor is it willingly accepting some outrageous misfortune as God's will. Rather, it means a willingness to die *in order to do God's revealed will.* Recently a man asked me to confirm a job he had taken that a Christian should not do. I told him that he was wrong to accept this job, and he said, "But I have to live, don't I?" My reply: "No! You do not have to live. We are called upon to take up a cross to follow Jesus."

Giving up one's life is certainly not rational or practical, at least apart from faith. But sound judgment within the framework of faith is a different matter. Orpah did the wise thing and Ruth the foolish from this world's perspective, but from the heavenly perspective and from the viewpoint of faith, Orpah played the fool and Ruth the wise woman. Orpah returned to her god, Chemosh, to whom she would sacrifice her firstborn. She lost her connection with the living God and His people. Ruth, however, by following her spiritual desires, gave birth to a son who was in the lineage of Jesus Christ. She enjoys forever a relationship with the living God and His people.

When we talk of sound judgment we mean within the framework of faith that to nonspiritual people seems irrational and impractical. Abraham received, as it were, his son back from the dead and became in God's sight the father of every believer, including you and me.

Unbelievers make sound judgment their first priority in making decisions; believers rely on God's Word. Obedience takes precedence over logic. With such a great resource at our disposal, we dare not neglect the counsel of God. Let us not live like those who do not know God.

Then, as the Lord guides us, we will make the best choices possible.

There are at least five things to consider when relying upon your own judgment.

## Decide in the Light of Scripture

When you rely on your own judgment, you do not want to negate anything in God's Word. On a number of occasions in Scripture the writer reveals his complete dependence upon the revealed Word of God. For instance, at the Jerusalem Council in Acts 15 James quotes Amos 9 before announcing, "It is my judgment, therefore, that we should not make it difficult for the Gentiles who are turning to God." He bases his judgment on the fact that the Scriptures reveal how Gentiles can be saved.

Paul and Barnabas preached the gospel in the Jewish synagogue of Pisidian Antioch, but were treated badly by jealous Jewish leaders. They responded by quoting the prophet Isaiah, saying, "We had to speak the word of God to you first. Since you reject it and do not consider yourselves worthy of eternal life, we now turn to the Gentiles. For this is what the Lord has commanded us: 'I have made you a light for the Gentiles, that you may bring salvation to the ends of the earth'" (Acts 13:46,47). After relying on Scripture, they made their decision.

Time after time Paul is found "reasoning from the Scriptures" with people. His letters are filled with reason based upon biblical principles. "So then," he says in 1 Thessalonians 5:6, since we are sons of light and do not belong to the night, "let us not be like others." This is a sound judgment made on the basis of biblical truth. Many times Paul concluded an argument by saying "Therefore," revealing his conclusion after offering God's truth.

God expects us to use sound judgment, but He never expects us to decide in opposition to the Bible. For example, Scripture is very clear about divorce. The Lord tells Malachi, "I hate divorce" (Malachi 2:16), and Jesus warned that "anyone who divorces his wife, except for marital unfaithfulness, causes her to commit adultery" (Matthew 5:32). Yet I know a Christian man who decided it was God's will that he divorce his wife. She had a mental illness, and he convinced himself that God wanted him to divorce her so that he could "go on in ministry." He had prayed about it and had decided this was the desire of his heart.

Unfortunately he received some terrible counsel from friends who justified his decision. He came to me about another matter, but in the course of our conversation, he told me about his plans to divorce his wife. I showed him what the Bible had to say about divorce, particularly the apostle Paul's entailments in 1 Corinthians 7. He had no biblical grounds to divorce his wife, yet this man responded to me by saying, "I know it's the right thing to do." He rejected God's Holy Word because of logic—his wife was unhealthy and he would be responsible.

As a matter of fact, he had already met the woman he was sure God wanted him to marry next. So he rejected the Word of the Lord, divorced his wife, and went on to lead divorce-recovery workshops in a local church. The man acted out of blatant disobedience and dishonor, but I hope he will repent and experience God's forgiveness. Nevertheless, the historical consequences of his divorce— the pain he inflicted upon his wife, his children, and himself—are just as real as those of a drunkard who, in his stupor, blinded a man. The drunkard hopefully will find God's forgiveness, but the man will be blind for the rest of his life.

An analogous situation occurred in the early church. The apostle Peter spent time living and eating with Gentile Christians in Antioch. He ate with them, worked with them, and lived as though he were not a Jew. The Lord had revealed to him in a vision that all food was acceptable, and that Christians no longer had to live according to the Old Testament dietary laws. But when the church in Jerusalem sent representatives to observe the situation in Antioch, Peter reasoned that he had better toe the line. So when the men from Jerusalem arrived, he stopped eating certain foods, began living like an Orthodox Jew, and separated himself from the Gentile Christians. Other Jewish believers, following Peter's lead, did the same.

The apostle Paul was living in Antioch at that time, and "when I saw that they were not acting in line with the truth of the gospel, I said to Peter in front of them all, 'You are a Jew, yet you live like a Gentile and not like a Jew. How is it, then, that you force Gentiles to follow Jewish customs?'" (Galatians 2:14). Paul saw that Peter was following human reason and disobeying God's Word. He was putting on a show for the benefit of the observers because he logically concluded that they would have harsh things to say about a Jew who lived as a Gentile. In doing so Peter rejected the Word of God as specially revealed to him. Christians can use sound judgment, but not at the expense of Scripture.

Human reasoning is a good thing and a gift from God. We ought to use it within the parameters of God's plan for guidance. But we should never resort to human logic in violation of the Bible. Instead, we use sound judgment in accordance with Scripture.

## Decide in the Light of Giftedness

Use sound judgment about yourself and your abilities. Take a look at the way the early church made the decision about who should wait on tables for the widows: "It would not be right for us to neglect the ministry of the word of God in order to wait on tables" (Acts 6:2,3). The apostles relied on sound judgment to make this decision. It would be a false humility to take the talents of the apostles and have them spend time feeding the widows at their tables. That is just not the best use of their apostolic gifts.

Paul said to the believers in Rome, "Do not think of yourselves more highly than you ought, but rather think of yourselves with sober judgment" (Romans 12:3). Each of us needs to consider how God has gifted us and how we should be using those gifts.

Paul had the gift of evangelism, so it made sense that he travel and preach the gospel to people who had never been exposed to the good news of Jesus Christ. Had Paul decided to simply remain a tentmaker in Antioch, he would not have been using his gifts to their fullest extent.

I know of a situation where a man with absolutely no musical giftedness longed to be in the music ministry of a church. I think he was enamored with the idea of being up front and having people applaud, so he continued trying out as a soloist, bringing his guitar to services, and generally pestering everyone to let him sing. The music minister, who had no idea what to do with a tone-deaf soloist, finally created a special "Monday music night" that featured this gentleman. It was, of course, a disaster. The same man later volunteered to do carpentry at the church, another area in which he had no giftedness. (The church body found it takes longer to fix a bad mistake than it does to do it right the first time!)

137

I share that story not to poke fun at the man's lack of musical and carpentry skills, but to point out that each person is gifted in an area that the church can use. This man clearly wanted to help people, and eventually the pastor found a perfect situation for him: helping transport the sick to their doctor appointments and taking meals to shut-ins. Each of us needs to determine our giftedness and serve in an area that uses our gift.

A friend of mine, an extremely shy man but a man with a heart for God, was asked to serve on the board of a high-profile nonprofit ministry. He really believed in the organization and its goals, but they asked him to spend his time raising funds for the ministry. They could have used that man in just about any other position, but the thought of talking to people scared him away. After considering their request, he had to turn them down. I appreciate a man who knows his own giftedness and doesn't let his ego carry him away. Before you make a major decision, consider the gifts God gave you. Do the ramifications of your decision match your gifts?

## Decide According to Your Ability

Know who you are. Evaluate your abilities and talents. Don't try to be what you're not, because if you do you will live in a constant state of anxiety. You'll always be afraid of being demoted. There are people who have advanced themselves beyond where the community has advanced them. They have put themselves in positions where they must try to be more than they can be.

Christians must know who they are, what their strengths and weaknesses are, and they must be content within those limitations. I like the lesson of Acts 11:29: "The disciples, each according to his ability, decided to provide help for the brothers living in Judea."

You can't give what you don't have. If you are not a teacher, do not sign up to teach a class; it will simply bore the students and upset your life. John Milton, wondering at his dimming eyesight, asked, "Does God require a day labor, light denied?" You must know what you can do.

I am a good lecturer, and students seem to enjoy taking my classes. My style and my voice are a good fit for an academic setting. But I'm not a pastor or an administrator. I'm just not skilled at these, nor do I have the desire to organize details, and more importantly I do not have the personality of a leader. I have been offered the position of president or dean of several theological schools, but I declined them. I had the good sense to recognize my deficiencies.

Moses had an incredible ability to lead people. Time after time he saved the nation of Israel by offering strong leadership in a most difficult situation. Although he was reluctant about getting started, he wound up being the greatest prophet Israel has ever known; a man "whom the LORD knew face to face, who did all those miraculous signs and wonders the LORD sent him to do in Egypt—to Pharaoh and to all his officials and to his whole land. For no one has ever shown the mighty power or performed the awesome deeds that Moses did in the sight of all Israel" (Deuteronomy 34:10-12). Moses was a man who knew his abilities.

It seems as though our Christian culture has become one of busyness. Most Christians are racing someplace every night of the week, filling their lives with activities. I wonder sometimes if they aren't wearing themselves out with activity because they don't have a mature spirituality. It takes a mature person to say no to another person, especially in the church. But a mature believer knows what his abilities are, and doesn't jump into a position merely because there is a need. We have to know both our skills and our limitations.

## Decide According to Your Circumstances

Again, we understand that human reason is last in line when it comes to making decisions. However, once we are sensitive to the guidance of God, we need to make decisions in His will according to our situation. Acts 9:23-25 tells of the Jewish plan to kill Paul: "But [Paul] learned of their plan. Day and night they kept close watch on the city gates in order to kill him. But his followers took him by night and lowered him in a basket through an opening in the wall." The friends of Paul used sound judgment in light of the circumstances. Knowing that the Lord was counting on using Paul in the future, they decided on a course of action that took into account the unique situation.

The apostle Paul was also faced with a difficult decision when he continued his ministry years later. He wanted to take Timothy along with him, but Timothy was the son of a Jewish mother and a Greek father, and Paul worried that the Jews would not accept him. "So he circumcised him because of the Jews who lived in that area, for they all knew that his father was a Greek" (Acts 16:3). Here is a case where the circumstances merited making a decision based on sound judgment.

When Paul was in the city of Ephesus he saw God do a mighty work. The Ephesian church was a vibrant body, and after the fall of Jerusalem it became the center of the Christian church. As Paul wrote to the believers in Corinth, he told them that he wanted to visit them, but he added, "After I go through Macedonia, I will come to you—for I will be going through Macedonia. Perhaps I will stay with you awhile, or even spend the winter, so that you can help me on my journey wherever I go. I do not want to see you now and make only a passing visit: I hope to spend some time with you, if the Lord permits. But I will stay on at Ephesus until Pentecost, because a great door for effective work has opened to me" (1 Corinthians 16:5-9). Notice how Paul was flexible, knowing that he was close to God and doing the work the Lord had called him to, so that he had the ability to change his schedule according to the circumstances.

We can see clearly how the decisions made in the New Testament differ from the means used in the Old Testament. How should Paul escape Jerusalem? Should he circumcise Timothy? Where should he go next year? Rather than cast a lot and expect God to answer miraculously, he based his decisions on sound judgment in light of the circumstances.

## Decide According to an Overall Strategy

Paul had an overall strategy for his life. He was headed north, through Galatia and Cappadocia, into Macedonia, and on to Bithynia. But it was at this point that he had a vision and God intervened in his plans. Still, Paul had a definite vision for his life, according to his heart's desire:

> Because I was confident of this, I planned to visit you first so that you might benefit twice. I planned to visit you on my way to Macedonia and to come back to you from Macedonia, and then have you send me on my way to Judea. When I planned this, did I do it lightly? Or do I make my plans in a worldly manner so that in the same breath I say "Yes, yes" and "No, no"? But as surely as God is faithful, our message to you is not "Yes" and "No." . . .
>
> I call God as my witness that it was in order to spare you that I did not return to Corinth. Not that we

lord it over your faith, but we work with you for your joy, because it is by faith you stand firm. So I made up my mind that I would not make another painful visit to you (2 Corinthians 1:15-18,23,24; 2:1).

Paul knew what he wanted to do and where he wanted to go. He had an overall strategy that he was working from, and that is an excellent idea for any mature believer. Have a plan; know what God wants you to do with your life. Then you will have a context for making long-term decisions. This will significantly improve your ability to make decisions in light of God's overall plan for your life.

We do not rely on our reasoning abilities to determine our course of action. As Christians we rely upon God's guidance. But as He leads we make decisions within His revealed will on the basis of sound judgment.

# DIVINE INTERVENTION

▼

*God does not intervene in response to seeking His will.*

CHAPTER 9

*I*N THINKING OUR WAY through God's program of guidance we should consider divine intervention as the last aspect. We take action first in reading and meditating upon God's Word, in following the desires of our heart, in listening to wise counsel, in considering God's providence, and, finally, in reasoning within the framework of our circumstances. God, however, may step into our lives and directly intervene apart from any action on our part. He is a God of miracles, and as Christians we must be open to the possibility that God will sovereignly intervene in our lives, though we do not depend on miracles to guide us, nor do we fail to act until one occurs.

*God does not intervene in response to seeking His will in a perplexing situation.* There are no examples of God stepping miraculously into the life of anyone in the New Testament in response to the seeking of His will. When the Lord does choose to do something miraculous, like sending a vision to Peter or transporting Philip to another town, it is not in response to a request for God to reveal His will. As a matter of fact, both of those men believed they were already doing God's will, and the Lord stepped in to change their situations. He has the power to step directly into our lives if He so chooses, and Christians must be ready this to happen at any time. But that is not normally how the Lord works, and it never seems to be the case that He intervenes due to a request for divine guidance in a particular situation. Divine intervention usually is limited to one of three roles: revealing a great truth, saving one of God's children from an intolerable situation, or revealing why a Christian should act in violation of God's normal program of guidance.

## Revealing a Great Truth

There were very few occasions in Scripture where the Lord stepped directly into the life of a believer to reveal some new truth. Christ met Saul on the road to Damascus and revealed Himself as the Messiah. It was an incredible situation, with Paul being knocked to the ground in a blaze of light and hearing the voice of Jesus speak directly to him.

However, we certainly cannot make Paul's conversion experience normative for all Christians. Most of us have never and will never speak to the Lord face-to-face while on this earth. If we used Paul's dramatic conversion as the model for all conversions, there would be very few people in the kingdom. Other disciples in the early church did not have this sort of conversion experience. There certainly is no history of God's people regularly experiencing anything like this in Christendom. So we must take it on faith that what happened to Paul was a unique experience, arranged by God to develop the greatest missionary of all time. Do not misunderstand me: God still gives His people visions and miraculously calls them to ministry at times.

There were other times when God miraculously intervened to reveal a great truth. He spoke with Peter as he prayed in Joppa, explaining that the Old Testament limitations on food were no longer in effect for Christians. He gave Paul a vision of heaven to encourage him, and John a vision of the end times to encourage all believers. In all three of these situations the Lord wanted to reveal a new truth about Himself, but in none of them were the men involved praying for God to supernaturally reveal His will.

## Salvation from an Intolerable Situation

Another situation in which divine intervention may occur is when the Lord wants to save one of His children from a dangerous situation. In Acts 12 we read about Peter being arrested by King Herod and remanded for public trial. Christians were praying earnestly for Peter, and "the night before Herod was to bring him to trial. Peter was sleeping between two soldiers, bound with two chains, and sentries stood guard at the entrance. Suddenly an angel of the Lord appeared and a light shone in the cell. He struck Peter on the side and woke him up. 'Quick, get up!' he said, and the chains fell off Peter's wrists. . . . They passed the first and second guards and came to the iron gate leading to the city. It opened for them by itself, and they went through it. When they had walked the length of one street, suddenly the angel left him" (Acts 12:6,7,10). A somewhat similar event occurred with Paul and Silas when they were arrested in Philippi (see Acts 16), and Paul's life was spared several times when he was on his missionary journeys. God certainly has the power to make the impossible happen. But that is not the way He *normally* works.

Paul was not always saved from punishment; many times he endured unjustified beatings. Once his friends had to let him over the city wall in a basket to save his life. James, the brother of John, was put to death by King Herod. Stephen was killed by a mob. "Some faced jeers and flogging, while still others were chained and put in prison. They were stoned; they were sawed in two: they were put to death by the sword. They went about in sheep-skins and goatskins, destitute, persecuted and mistreated" (Hebrews 11:36,37). All too often a story or verse of Scripture has been used out of context to normalize divine intervention, causing some Christians to believe that God will *always* intervene physically on behalf of His children. That is just not true, though He has at times done so.

## Overriding God's Program of Guidance

The third occasion in which the Lord will divinely intervene is when He wants to reveal why a Christian should act in violation of His normal program of guidance. This does not happen often, and I can't find any biblical examples of it happening in response to someone praying for God to reveal His will in a specific situation. But He does occasionally intervene to change the course of our lives.

*Sometimes the Lord will act to change our perspective of Scripture.* We are people of the ear, not of the eye, and so we live by His Word. The Bible is the first place we go to get His guidance. But there have been a few situations where the Lord supernaturally intervened to change our perspective of Scripture.

When God changed from administering His people from under the Old Covenant to under the New, He inter-vened in a supernatural way. When the Lord wanted to change the dietary laws for His people, He gave Peter an unexpected vision. Peter was praying on the roof of his home, when suddenly God gave him a vision of a sheet falling from heaven containing all kinds of animals. A voice told him, "Get up, Peter. Kill and eat." Now at this point in his life Peter was a good Jew. He followed the dietary restrictions of the Old Testament dietary law, not eating the meat of reptile or animals that had a cloven hoof. So he responded by saying, "Surely not, Lord! I have never eaten anything impure or unclean" (Acts 10:14). But the voice told him, "Do not call anything impure that God has made clean." The vision was repeated twice more, and immediately afterward Peter was given a chance to minister to a God-fearing Gentile. The Lord used this incident as a means of teaching Peter that Christians, even Jewish Christians, were no longer living under the dietary laws of the Old Covenant.

This was significant change in God's administration. Peter had read his Bible, followed his heart, and received counsel from others, and he was living according to his best judgment. All the other elements of God's program of guidance were in operation, so God had to intervene dramatically to make this change. Without this sort of dramatic, supernatural act the church might never have come to this conclusion on its own. God was making a significant alteration in the lives of His people, so He used divine intervention to teach them the new way of things.

Notice that Peter was not seeking the Lord's will on this matter. For him, the issue was closed. As a good Jew he knew that he must live according to the law. God's intervention was necessary to radically alter his perspective. The Lord even had to show it to Peter three times before it got into his head that God was changing things!

This does not mean that we can allow anyone claiming a message from God to alter our view of Scripture. These are dangerous waters, for we clearly should never go against the teaching of the New Testament. But the early church had to know that as Christians we are under a New Covenant, and God rules our world with a different administration from that of the Old Testament. When the Lord changed the administration of His people, there had to be a direct revelation to the apostles. This sort of divine intervention is not applicable to us today because we live under the New Testament, the Canon of Scripture is complete, and God has made His Word clear. He has set His administration in place for the church age. Anything that is not in conformity with this standard for the church's faith and practice is anathema. But this was not true in the early church, and to educate them to the new way of things, the Lord had to intervene in a special way.

*Sometimes the Lord wants to change our perspective of heartfelt desire.* Paul had a heartfelt desire to take the gospel to the area known in the Roman Empire as Bithynia, but God intervened to stop him. He was at Troas, in what is now northwest Turkey, making plans to head north with his companions, when God gave him a vision: "During the night Paul had a vision of a man of Macedonia standing and begging him, 'Come over to Macedonia and help us.' After Paul had seen the vision, we got ready at once to leave for Macedonia, concluding that God had called us to preach the gospel to them" (Acts 16:9,10).

Paul knew exactly what he wanted to do, but the Lord had other plans and actually intervened to change Paul's direction. Instead of going north into Bithynia, he went west into Europe, arriving at Philippi and meeting some women at a prayer meeting. That was the beginning of the church in the Western world. It all began when Paul talked with seven women at a river outside Philippi, a city he never intended to visit. The Lord had to tell Paul of a new direction for his life, for Paul had made other plans.

God did the same thing with Moses, interrupting his life through a burning bush and getting him back into national leadership rather than tending sheep in a foreign land. Occasionally the Lord will turn a person toward a completely new objective—but keep in mind that historically He did so only in matters of the utmost importance, and He did more than just give the person a "feeling." The Lord actually appeared and spoke directly to him about the importance of his new task.

*The Lord may intervene to change our perspective of wise counsel and sound judgment.* Sometimes the Lord will directly intervene in a Christian's life when He requires them to do something that wise counselors or sound judgment would warn of. For example, the elders at Ephesus really did not want Paul traveling to Jerusalem in Acts 20. They knew his life was in danger in that city. The prophet even warned that Paul would be bound and handed over to the Gentiles. But Paul told those men he was "compelled by the Spirit" to return to Jerusalem. Wise counsel suggested that he stay in Ephesus, but God insisted he return to Jerusalem.

Philip is another early Christian who loved the Lord Jesus and wanted to tell others about Him. He lived in Jerusalem at the start of the church age—a place where many people were coming to know Christ. He was an effective evangelist with a knack for talking to people. It made absolutely no sense for Philip to leave a great evangelistic opportunity to go to one lone individual. It was totally against sound judgment. So it required the Spirit's intervention for Philip to travel down the road to Gaza in order to meet one man. By all accounts Philip should have stayed where he was, but God intervened: "Now an angel of the Lord said to Phillip, 'Go south to the road—the desert road—that goes down from Jerusalem to Gaza.' So he started out, and on his way he met an Ethiopian eunuch ..." (Acts 8:26,27). It was not sound judgment for Philip to make that change, but in God's overall plan He needed Philip to talk to that eunuch.

## Listening to the Guidance of God

The common idea of divining God's will is either a pagan notion that we Christians need to let go of or a mode of administration that God no longer uses. God has given us a program of guidance that involves getting to know Him through His Word and letting Him shape our character, our hearts, and our desires. Then as we know the mind of God we can live out His will. He expects us to first draw close to Him, then allows for seeking wise counsel as confirmation, or taking our circumstances into consideration and using our own sound judgment to make a decision. He never calls us in the New Testament to "seek His will," but rather to seek His kingdom and do His will. *We ought to stamp out of our vocabulary the nonbiblical and misleading expression "finding God's will."* Rather than talk about "seeking the will of God," we ought to speak of following the *guidance* of God. This is not just semantically different, since He is calling us to draw close to Himself and to live holy lives. God's will for us is that we be holy; there is no mystery to His will. As for those questions about changing jobs, getting married, going to school, and the like, finding answers will require growing close to God.

We must learn to listen to God as the Spirit speaks to us through His Word. The framework of faith, it bears repeating, is not always humanly rational. We have to listen to God when He tells us to do something that, at first blush, sounds sort of crazy. Abraham listened when God called Him to sacrifice his son. Joshua listened when the Lord called him to march his army around the city walls of Jericho blowing trumpets and shouting. Gideon in spite of his cowardice, finally listened when God told him to go into battle against a vast army with only 300 men. As the people of God have allowed the Holy Spirit to speak to them, we recognize that God's guidance may not always seem rational. As we read and meditate on His Word, and our hearts burn within us, we can count on the Holy Spirit giving us direction. He may challenge us to do mighty exploits for Him.

## Are You Obedient?

God honors obedience. He is in your life, ready to lead you according to His program of guidance. But He cannot lead a person who does not listen to Him, who is not close to Him. If you are struggling with a specific question, rather than trying to magically divine God's answer, spend time drawing close to Him. Then your character, and perhaps your perspective, will change. Then God will shape your desires. Then you will have the mind of Christ.

Ask yourself if your motivation in life is to glorify God. Often the struggles we have with situations do not grow out of love for God, but out of selfishness and pride.

Not long ago I had a long conversation with a young man who had all sorts of questions about "God's will for his life." He wanted to know which job he should have, which school he should attend, which neighborhood he should live in, which car he should purchase—his list went on and on.

My response to him was simply, "What's your motivation?"

He didn't understand my question. He wanted a simple answer, a magic formula for divining the mind of the Almighty. I told him that didn't exist, but that if he would examine his motivation, he would see that his perspective was all wrong. All of his questions were about how he could benefit; none were about how he could obey. I encouraged him to think about what the Bible has to say about God's will. It tells us clearly that God wants us to be holy. The Lord wants us mature. That is clearly the most important lesson given to Christians in the New Testament.

I asked that young man who his god is. Is it the Almighty God, who created us and in love sent His Son to die on the cross for us? Or is it personal success, with the right car, the perfect home, and the ideal job? God is more interested in my holiness than in my success. That young man wondered out loud how God would lead us if we didn't ask Him to reveal His will.

So I described God's pattern for guidance to him, and I could see he finally was beginning to understand. It takes a whole new frame of reference to think this way, and it means letting go of a philosophical construct most of us have grown up with in the church. Eventually he seemed to grasp what I was saying. God is leading clearly. We all know that His desire for us is that we become like Jesus Christ. But that takes hard work, total devotion, and a commitment to serve God's purposes rather than our own. That's hard to do, and I'm not sure most Christians are ready for that message. But that's what God's will is for each of us.

> The God who made the world and everything in
> it is the Lord of heaven and earth. . . . From one man
> he made every nation of men, that they should

inhabit the whole earth; and he determined the times set for them and the exact places where they should live. *God did this so that men would seek him and perhaps reach out for him and find him, though he is not far from each one of* us. "For in him we live and move and have our being." As some of your own poets have said, "We are his offspring." Therefore since we are God's offspring, we should no think that the divine being is like gold or silver or stone—an image made by man's design and skill. In the past God overlooked such ignorance, but now he commands all people everywhere to repent. For he has set a day when he will judge the world with justice by the man he has appointed. He has given proof of this to all men by raising him from the dead (Acts 17:24-31).

*I don't doubt that the Holy Spirit guides your decisions from within when you make them with the intention of pleasing God. The error would be to think that He speaks only within, whereas in reality He speaks also through Scripture, the Church, Christian friends, books etc.*

LETTERS OF C. S. LEWIS
(20 JUNE 1952)

# AFTERWORD

*W*HY WOULD A GOD who wants us to do His will hide it from us? Why do Christians go through such convoluted, painful efforts to know it? His will needn't be hidden or elusive; a mystery, a puzzle, an enigma. The answer we seek already lies in our theology—what we believe.

Our lives and our character ought to be changed by what we believe. And when our lives are changed, we are transformed into His likeness. The concept is very simple: Don't you think we will be better able to understand His will when we are more like Him?

My career in theological education has been to direct Christians to understand that God calls us, compels us, and provides for us a character-transforming response. Understanding your theology provides clear direction for God's will in your life, with no smoke and mirrors, no guessing or gambling.

But, in sharing with you my thoughts about finding His will for your life, it's important for you to understand something about our theology. Why is it true? Why is it essential? Why should it be my way of life?

As we address these three questions you'll be ready to begin what I pray will be your last quest to understand God's will for your life.

**1. Theology is truth.** Sound theology involves propositions about divine matters. If a theological institution is worth its salt it must be committed to truth, which involves in part linking words to realities. Theology sets forth the content of divine realities in propositional form. Truth ultimately pertains to a correlation between behavior and these ultimate realities, but the Bible makes many assertions about God, His intervention in our world, human behavior, and the human situation before a holy God. Moses referred to the correspondence between reality and words as "law." The New Testament writers referred to them as "doctrine." Today, we generally call it "theology."

Ever since the Enlightenment, the Western world has held a faith in the power of the human mind and of the scientific method to know "truth." It has sought to understand and control nature and has believed, almost without question, that anything that could not be understood by unaided human reason and validated by science was not to be taken seriously. We can know absolutely, however, only if we know comprehensively. To make an absolute judgment, according to Cornelius Van Til, humanity must usurp God's throne:

> If one does not make human knowledge wholly dependent upon the original self-knowledge and consequent revelation of God to man, then man will have to seek knowledge within himself as the final reference point. Then he will have to seek an exhaustive

understanding of reality. He will have to hold that if he cannot attain to such an exhaustive understanding of reality, he has no true knowledge of anything at all. Either man must then know everything or he knows nothing. This is the dilemma that confronts every form of non-Christian thinking.[4]

A play does not make sense if you view only the first act. It is not until the final act, when the last words are spoken and the curtain drops, that the play takes on its full meaning. Humans are confined to the tensions of the middle acts; without revelation, they are not privy to their resolution in the final act. This partiality condemns itself. It makes all the difference in the world whether good or evil will finally triumph or go on indefinitely in an unresolved stalemate. Without revelation, humanity cannot answer the fundamental questions of its existence.

The human mind, employing the scientific method, can certainly determine the "truthfulness" of statements pertaining to empirical data, whether or not they cohere with the physical world. That method can answer questions of proximate origins ("How did X arise out of Y?"), but it cannot answer the question of ultimate origins ("How did the law governing X arising out of Y originate?"). Theology deals with what we call "First Cause," the beginning of all things. Science deals with second causality, and is restricted to finite factors. Scientific methods got man to the moon by overcoming its ignorance of physical laws, but once a man stood on the moon, the mystery of humanity's existence on earth became even more profound. Science answers questions with as much mathematical precision as possible; questions about the "when" and "how" of this finite world. But science cannot overcome mystery. It cannot decide ultimate meaning and without that light establish a credible ethic. As Albert Einstein once put it. "The function of setting up goals and passing statements of value transcends the domain of science."

Since unaided human reason and the scientific method cannot validate ultimate truth, many modern scholars deny its existence. The presupposition of the Enlightenment leads to agnosticism. It leaves humanity only with valuations, what certain people at certain times have thought to be good, but without values—that which is eternally good. According to this point of view we can be certain only that the meanings and values embraced by one generation will be discarded by the next.

Yet this presupposition confronts the human spirit with a contradiction: we yearn for absolute certainty, meaning, and values. We desire truth. All human beings want to see things holistically and within that frame of reference to commit themselves to something enduring. "He has also set eternity in the hearts of men," says the Teacher in Ecclesiastes 3:11, "yet they cannot fathom what God has done from the beginning to end." The fact is that the Holy Spirit offers conviction that the Bible is truth.

By showing the inadequacy of unaided human reason I have sought to establish negatively and indirectly the necessity of divine revelation, a proposition that means God is there and that He has spoken. It is well known that the Bible claims to be the Word of God, but what is not as well known is that the truthfulness of the Bible depends on the convicting work of the Holy Spirit and not on human reason. 'My conviction that the Bible can be trusted as God's Word does not come from human reason, but from the Holy Spirit. If Scripture's claim to truth must be validated by finite, fallible human reason, then even if it is inspired revelation of truth, humanity cannot know it and must continue to despair of attaining the meaning and value they seek. The Holy Spirit revealed the truth, to the extent God was pleased to make it known, inspired its expression in Scripture, and bears witness to its truthfulness. Throughout history the church has heard the voice of God in Scripture (see John 10:3-6; 2 Corinthians 3:14-18; and 1 Thessalonians 2:13). The *Scots Confession* articulately expressed that truth in 1560 with the words,

> Our faith and its assurance do not proceed from flesh and blood, that is to say, from natural powers within us, but are the inspiration of the Holy Ghost: whom we confess to be God, equal with the Father and with His Son, who sanctifies us, and brings us into all truth by His own working, without whom we should remain forever enemies to God and ignorant of His Son, Christ Jesus. For by nature we are so deaf, blind, and perverse, that neither can we feel when we are pricked, see the light when it shines, nor assent to the will of God when it is revealed, unless the Spirit of the Lord Jesus quicken that which is dead, remove the darkness from our minds, and bow our stubborn hearts to the obedience of His blessed will.[5]

Calvin in his justly famous *Institutes,* wrote:

> The testimony of the Spirit is more excellent than all reason. For as God alone is a fit witness of Himself in His Word, so also the Word will not find acceptance in men's hearts before it is sealed by the inward testimony of the Spirit. The same Spirit, therefore, who has spoken through the mouths of the prophets must penetrate into our hearts to persuade us that they faithfully proclaimed what had been divinely commanded.[6]

Christian knowledge and understanding are grounded in God's revelation in the Bible through the Holy Spirit, who revealed the truth and illuminates its meaning. Humans cannot manipulate this process. We join with Paul in praying, "I keep asking that the God of our Lord Jesus Christ, the glorious Father, may give you the Spirit of wisdom and revelation, so that you may know him better. I pray also that the eyes of your heart may be enlightened in order that you may know the hope to which he has called you, the riches of his glorious inheritance in the saints, and his incomparably great power for us who believe" (Ephesians 1:17-19). Theology is truth, and passing on that truth to the next generation is part of the mission of the church. To achieve this mission it is dependent on the Holy Spirit. Furthermore, the church has reflected on this revelation for two millennia and given it expression in creeds and writings. If we are to know God and His will, it will be in the context of the Father sharing His truth with us.

**2. Theology is an essential part of spiritual formation.** In theological circles people speak of "exegesis"—constructing some accredited method to get out of the written text what the original author intended. If we accept the concept that the Holy Spirit plays a determinative role in revealing truth, then we must also concede that the Holy Spirit must be an essential part of our lives if we are to correctly read and interpret Scripture.

Unfortunately, many Christians seem to divorce theology from spirituality. I have seen seminary faculties divided over this issue, with those teaching spirituality courses fearing that those who teach exegesis will subvert the student's faith, and those teaching exegesis suspicious of their counterparts for not relying enough on the originally intended meaning of the Bible.

Historically, orthodox theologians confess that the Holy Spirit must illumine the Bible's meaning. "No one knows the thoughts of God except the Spirit of God," says Paul in 1 Corinthians 2:11. The apostle argues that only as we are in step with the Spirit can we know the things of God. "For if God does not open and explain Holy Writ," Martin Luther commented, "no one can understand it." Similarly, John Calvin in the Catechism of the Church of Geneva wrote:

> Our mind is too weak to comprehend the spiritual wisdom of God which is revealed to us by faith, and our hearts are too prone either to defiance or to a perverse confidence in ourselves or creaturely things. But the Holy Spirit enlightens us to make us capable of understanding what would otherwise be incomprehensible to us, and fortifies us in certitude, sealing and imprinting the promises of salvation on our hearts.[7]

In our modern day, the Chicago Statement of Faith continues the tradition: "The Holy Spirit, Scripture's divine author, both authenticates it to us by His inward witness and opens our minds to understand its meaning."[8] Yet I find that most modern Bible scholars subscribe to the idea intellectually while ignoring it in practice. Almost any textbook on hermeneutics or Bible interpretation written by an evangelical during the past twenty years emphasizes finding the meaning of the original language in its historical context while neglecting to mention the role of the Holy Spirit and His impact on the life of the interpreter. My own teaching has been flawed by the same imbalance. A student once asked me about the relationship of the

Spirit's illumination and the grammatical-historical method of interpreting Scripture, and I was so dull I had to admit I had not even thought of the question!

The Reformers carefully balanced being a language and historical student with being a spiritual man or woman. Yet modern theologians, perhaps due to the influence of the Enlightenment, diminish the role of the Holy Spirit in understanding Scripture. J.A. Ernesti, one of the clearest and most influential theologians of the last century, felt that a Christian can understand God's Word without resorting to prayer. According to him, "Pious simplicity of mind is useless in the investigation of Scriptural truth." That sort of attitude denies the proper role of the Spirit in the life of the believer. I have heard excellent exegesis at the annual Society of Biblical Literature seminars, but I've never heard a prayer offered at that learned society.

There is a profound difference between head knowledge and heart knowledge. Intellectually comprehending the truth of Scripture is just not the same as appropriating its truths. Moreover, it cannot be understood appropriately without a spiritual commitment. Bible study requires a personal relationship with the Divine author if it is to be fully understood. Second Timothy 3:16 suggests that Scripture involves three objects at the same time: God, the inspired author, and the text. Note that only the last of these is impersonal. One may distance oneself from an impersonal text, but to fully know a person requires passion; one must commit oneself to another.

*Our theology, therefore, needs to lead us into an encounter with God.* Through the inspired author's text God aimed to disclose Himself. The text was never intended as an end in itself, which is why Solomon boldly combined his teaching with knowing God: "My son, if you accept my words . . . then you will find the knowledge of God" (Proverbs 2:1-5).

The words "knowledge of God" is the Hebrew word for "theology," the study of divine things. It transcends intellectual understanding, and refers to the involvement of the total personality with God. As John Frame puts it:

> Listening to Scripture is not merely a transaction between ourselves and a book, even a very extraordinary book; rather, in Scripture we meet God Himself. For Protestant (at least those outside charismatic circles), no experience offers a more profound closeness with God.[9]

Theology, what we know about God, changes our lives. We approach God's Word spiritually and personally.

Then too, to understand the human, inspired author, a reader must come to meet him with empathy. Without empathy we cannot understand the author. An unsympathetic reader distorts an author's meaning.

In a question period that followed a lecture on Genesis 3 by my Harvard professor, who taught me much about the biblical text, a student pushed him to identify the "seed of the serpent," the "seed of the woman," and the nature of their antipathy. To my astonishment my respected professor interpreted the text with such crass literalness that, according to him, the passage presented in mythical form the eternal antipathy between snakes and mankind, nothing more. I wondered how such an interpretation was possible. Obviously the fast-talking serpent is extraordinary—it talked, was diabolical, and knew of heavenly matters. My professor missed the text's meaning, I suggest, because he lacked spiritual empathy with its author.

Paul, writing in Romans 1, reminds us that due to our innate depravity, we fail to grasp God, we suppress the truth, and we justify our unethical conduct. Satan deceives us with half-truths. Sin has destroyed our ability to do what is right. Thus, apart from God's regeneration and the work of the Holy Spirit, we cannot hear the text clearly or allow it to shape our lives.

The very nature of God demands that the theology student has proper spiritual qualifications. God has sovereignly revealed Himself in Scripture. We cannot make Him talk through the scientific method. As David Steinmetz says:

> Scripture is not in our power. It is not at the disposal of our intellect and is not obligated to render up its secrets to those who have theological training merely because they are learned. Scripture imposes its own meaning; it binds the soul to God through faith. Because the initiative in the interpretation of Scripture remains in the hands of God, we must humble ourselves in His presence and pray that He will give understanding and wisdom to us as we meditate on the sacred text. While we may take courage from the thought that God gives understanding of Scripture to the humble, we should also heed the warning that the truth of God can never coexist with human pride. Humility is the hermeneutical precondition for authentic exegesis.[10]

When Jesus walked among the people, most thought He was a great prophet. Yet when Peter confessed Him to be the Son of the living God, Christ said, "This was not revealed to you by man, but by my Father in heaven" (Matthew 16:17). Peter understood the truth of Jesus, the "theology" of Christ, because he was in relationship with God, and God revealed it to him.

**3. Theology is a way of life.** If truth is a correspondence between expression and reality, then our behavior, our lifestyle, needs to correspond to our words. As the military puts it, "Don't just talk the talk; walk the walk." To be sure we need sound propositions of truth, but these ultimately serve to assure sound behavior. God tells us about Himself so that we can live in His truth. Knowing God, which we inadequately refer to as "theology," designates more than the involvement of a personality in the presence of the Lord. God is known through doing His will. One author put it: "the knowledge of God is defined throughout as obedience to His will." [11]

The Bible consistently demands action, not words. God was pleased to validate His own character in the acid test of history. He was not content with merely propositional truths about Himself. That's why Jesus draws His famous Sermon on the Mount to its conclusion with these sobering words: "Therefore every one who hears these words of mine and puts them into practice is like a wise man who built his house on the rock" (Matthew 7:24). Jesus commends the preaching of the teachers of the law, but condemns them for failing to practice what they preached. He went on to say that on the day of judgment, we will be judged by our works, not our words.

The quintessential expression of biblical ethics is to "do to others as you would have them do to you" (Matthew 7:12). Christianity thinks of itself as a *faith,* but Scripture suggests that God's people will follow not just a faith but a *way,* a life path. The word "faith" refers to the believer's faithfulness to the Lord, not merely to the belief system. The book of Proverbs uses that metaphor of "the way" seventy times, and the Lord Jesus referred to Himself as "the way, the truth, and the life." The "way" denotes a traversable road, leading to a destination. It also suggests the course of life for Christians.

If we are committed to the "way" of Jesus Christ, a way that compels the transformation of lives and cultures into a conformity with the ultimate realities of God, our theology (what we believe about God) will shape our lives (how we live for God). As we are led by the Spirit into a fuller understanding of Him, we experience what Scripture calls "the will of God."

# NOTES

1. William Evans, *The Great Doctrines of the Bible* (Moody, 1974), p. 17.

2. Michael De Robertis, quoted in *The Globe and Mail* (Canada), November 17, 1992.

3. For a thorough exploration of our culture's fascination with divination and alleged spiritual phenomena, see *Mind Games* by André Kole and Jerry MacGregor (Eugene, OR: Harvest House Publishers, 1998).

4. Cornelius Van Til, *A Christian Theory of Knowledge* (Philadelphia: Presbyterian and Reformed, n.d.), p. 17.

5. "The Scots Confession," Presbyterian Church U.S.A., *The Book of Confessions* (New York and Atlanta: Office of the General Assembly, 1983), vol. 3, p. 12.

6. John Calvin, *Institutes of the Christian Religion,* Book 1, vol. 7, p. 4.

7. John Calvin, *The Catechism of the Church of Geneva,* vol. 1, p. 7.

8. Short statement number 3, from J.I. Packer, *God Has Spoken* (Toronto: Hodder and Stoughton, 1979), p. 143.

9. John Frame, *Spiritual Formation* (Philadelphia: Westminster Press, 1981), p. 221.

10. David Steinmetz, "Who Is God?", p. 28.

11. Brevard Childs, *Old Testament Theology in a Canonical Context* (Philadelphia: Fortress Press, 1986), p. 51.